The Instructional Soul

The Instructional Soul

Leading Schools with a Spirit of Innovation

Daniel J. Evans

ROWMAN & LITTLEFIELD
Lanham • Boulder • New York • London

Published by Rowman & Littlefield
An imprint of The Rowman & Littlefield Publishing Group, Inc.
4501 Forbes Boulevard, Suite 200, Lanham, Maryland 20706
www.rowman.com

6 Tinworth Street, London SE11 5AL

Copyright © 2019 by Daniel J. Evans

All rights reserved. No part of this book may be reproduced in any form or by any electronic or mechanical means, including information storage and retrieval systems, without written permission from the publisher, except by a reviewer who may quote passages in a review.

British Library Cataloguing in Publication Information Available

Library of Congress Cataloging-in-Publication Data Available

ISBN 978-1-4758-4954-7 (cloth : alk. paper)
ISBN 978-1-4758-4955-4 (pbk. : alk. paper)
ISBN 978-1-4758-4956-1 (electronic)

Contents

Preface		vii
Acknowledgments		ix
1	The Boy in the Back Row	1
2	Discovering Our Souls	19
3	The "So What" of Systems Change	45
4	A Path to Self-Actualization	69
5	The Possibilities of Community	87
6	A Roadmap for Evolving Systems	107
7	It's the Ecology, Stupid	121
Afterword: A Note on Leadership		135
References		141
About the Author		143

Preface

I have a soul. Of this, I am certain.

I cannot tell you how I know this or how it came to be, but I know it without question. I can only tell you that there is a deep certainty of faith buried somewhere beneath my conscience that drives all that I do. On a wide continuum of stuff that I cannot explain nor measure, this soul of mine, this deep faith of which I speak, might be described by others as core values, beliefs, or morals.

As I am neither a preacher nor a philosopher, I will leave those distinctions to others. What I know for certain is that this soul of mine shapes my actions as a husband, father, teacher, and leader. It grounds my decisions. It undergirds my intellect. It forms my personality and shapes my humanity.

This is not to suggest that having a soul means that I make wise decisions, nor that I always manage my life in ways that serve a greater purpose. Still, it does mean that I tend to make *consistent* decisions and that I remain *focused*, in large part because I *attempt* to serve a greater purpose. To get closer to the point of this text, it is important to know that this soul of mine drives my life's work as an educator.

My personal reality aside, let me be clear from the start that this book is not about me in any way. It is actually about you. It is about our schools and the dedicated leaders who serve them. It is about the intriguing possibilities available to each of us, if only we were bold enough to install in our schools a stronger sense of purpose, a meaningful alignment of our work, and the capacity to inspire all children. In the end, this is a systems book, one that dares some new thoughts about how we might view our schools and communities in building systems that are so unlike what we have now that you may resist some of the ideas at first. That is certainly okay.

I began the work of constructing this text with a great deal of self-reflection and some deep meditation regarding what *might* be if anything *could* be. Yes, this text was a long time in the making. It is the kind of book that one cannot write until he has lived a little, wrestled with the ideas of others, tried some of his own, failed several times, read a lot, prayed a lot, learned some, loved some, gotten lost in indecision and regret, been smitten by the promise of hope and ambition, and then been torn aghast by the grim realities of time, space, capacity, and even bureaucracy in realizing that the possibilities are still many though the accomplishments are few.

Still, I am writing this book now knowing that our industry needs a fresh commentary every now and then, that my life and work experiences have been varied and dense enough, and my studies enriching and devout enough, to offer a modest proposal to the dedicated educators who serve our schools each day. In fact, let it be known that many of us still believe that our schools and the compassionate educators who serve our children are the key agents for every good thing there ever was and for all good things to come.

Like you, I have spent most of my life as a teacher and leader of children in our public schools and I have lived a lifetime in between. I spent ten years as a high school English teacher, first as the world's worst first-year teacher and later as a veteran educator with enough tactics and resolve to teach any sixteen-year-old how to write. I have spent the past fifteen years as a school and district leader, including five awesome years as the principal of the school where I was once a sixteen-year-old who couldn't write.

In between, I have been married to the same woman, had myself a kid and a couple of pets, stared down several bills that I could not pay, forged some deep wounds that are still not healed, and uncovered my soul through a rich exposure of life and death. Still, none of this makes me the appropriate spokesperson for a book on systems change.

Except for this.

Though I am not a wise old man, though I am no sage, and certainly no prophet, I can promise you that I have a soul that is a long time in the making and still a work in progress. And then there's this. Though I continue to search for answers, I can finally say, without equivocation, that I know all of the questions. Yes, finally, I know the questions. And that makes me like you and everyone else, in an upright and perfect posture to dare a book like this one and offer it up to others.

Acknowledgments

The inspiration for a book like this one does not come only from within. It is breathed into existence through subtle whisperings and clever rants offered by colleagues and students amid crowded cafeterias and noisy hallways over many school years. The conclusions are derived from a lifetime of restless disputations with so many exceptional teachers that I could never name them all here. I remain grateful to each and every one of them in every school I have served.

The same hearty appreciation is afforded the top-notch principals and district leaders with whom I have worked and toiled to find the right remedies in fixing what pains our educational system. I hope that the ideas provided in this text draw on our shared victories and collective missteps, and that they honor the sacrifice of our good deeds.

Among the wide expanse of ideas and manuscripts floating about the universe, I am grateful that this one landed delicately on the desk of Ms. Sarah Jubar at Rowman & Littlefield. Thank you, Sarah, for supporting this project from the start. It gives me hope to know that the world is still on the lookout for new ideas and that some people are still willing to gamble on one.

Though we have been adults for too long now, I would like to offer a belated thank you to my college friends who joined me all those years ago in dedicating our lives to the high ideals of an imperfect democracy and to the serious matter of putting compelling words to proper thoughts.

Finally, I cannot thank my wife (Judy) and son (Connor) enough for their unwavering support over many weekends and late nights. I have come to learn that the book never mattered much to them. It was me they cared about. To this day, they remain steadfast in providing me space when needed and prodding when required. In addition to all of that, they brought forward some occasional tough love, some well-played sarcasm, and the unabashed affection that only a family can provide.

Yes, everybody's story needs a hero, and they remain the heroes of my life epic.

Chapter One

The Boy in the Back Row

He has no name. Only a number.

He sits quietly each day in his seat in the back row, the one the teacher assigned to him. He did not choose this classroom nor this seat. They chose him. The desk next to him is open. The one in front of him is taken by a girl with soft skin. He knows the girl well from the back, for he has gotten lost many times in the rich darkness of her long, straight hair.

The teacher seems nice, though he does not know her name and she does not know his. She talks a lot, but her words make little sense to him. Some in the classroom nod their heads when she speaks. Others just look down. The teacher doesn't look his way much, though she has asked him for answers before. He is quick to tell her that he has none to offer. And now she asks him less. The teacher says they are learning a lot, and he trusts that she is right. He finds the things he learns in school are not like the things he learns at home.

The teacher does not know the students' names, though she did assign them numbers. She made the students memorize them and repeat them back to her. The boy wishes that his teachers knew him better. If they did, they would know that he doesn't talk much but that he is a kind person and that he wants to learn. He wants to be smart like them. If they knew him, they would know that he is named after his grandfather, a giant of a man who whiled away his days in the bowels of the Pennsylvania steel mills, there among the ash and fire that darkened the waterfront, polluted his lungs, and built this school and this desk.

If the teachers knew him, they would know that school and books and homework are not something that his mom and he talk about at home as much as they talk about paying the light bill. They would know that his dad was raised as a lean and hearty roughneck in the small boroughs that surround the steel mills. They would know that he smoked cheap cigarettes and drank beer from a can until the day he died. They would know that the boy is strong like his father.

If his teachers knew him, they would know that he can catch a ball better than any boy on the street. That he can take apart just about anything and put it back together again. That he started his own lawn business last summer and that he mows seven of them on the weekends. That he saved up $517 before his mom spent most of it. If the teachers knew him, they would know that he is tired. Though he is not yet a man, he is always, always tired.

If the teachers knew him, they would know that he stays up late, waiting for his mom and stepdad to stop fighting. That he lies there with the lights turned off, and that he dreams the lives of others, and that he pretends not to hear the door slam in the other room, the smell of cigarettes under his door. They would know that he is not old enough to drive but that he can keep a car straight on the road, late at night, by holding his stepdad's shoulders steady from the back seat. They would know why he is so tired.

If his teachers knew him better, they would know that the boy wishes he were like the other boys, the ones in the front row. Because *they* would know that *he* knows that the other boys are not any smarter than him. The teacher just calls on them more. For now, the boy is content to survive school until they tell him that he doesn't have to go anymore, and he wonders if the school is just trying to survive him.

He wishes it were not so.

In the meantime, he remains quiet and out of sight, there in the back row. Somehow, it feels safer that way, dreaming the lives of others and staring at a girl whose name he does not know.

LESSONS FROM THE BOY IN THE BACK ROW

As teachers and leaders in school systems across the globe, we have much to learn from the boy in the back row. Though some will argue passionately that our schools and the lessons we teach are successful in reaching most children, the evidence is not as convincing. As much as it hurts us to admit it, every study, survey, and statistic there ever was tells us that the boy in the back row is not the exception but is like too many children across too many schools.

This is not to say that our students will not graduate, find jobs, and raise families. Most of them do. It is not to say that our students will not learn in the system we have provided them, nor that they will not make friends, laugh a little, live a little, and mature along the way. For we all do. Still, what is lost in all of this chatter about educating children from all backgrounds is the uncomfortable reality that many of our students are underserved, underchallenged, and underinspired by a system that is overregulated, overburdened, and overwhelmed.

While it is not true that the boy in the back row is learning *in spite of us*, it is fair to wonder if he is learning *less* than he is capable of *because of us*. You see, the boy himself is a paradox. He is outwardly quiet, compliant, and on track to graduate, while inside he is clamoring for so much more. He seeks to be inspired by the system we have provided him. Like each of us, he longs for attention and acceptance, love and respect, creative expression, deep understanding, and rich discourse that can only arise from authentic relationships and meaningful experiences. The system promises him these things, though it doesn't always deliver.

As we untangle the reasons why this is, we must question whether our schools and school systems are unaware of this boy's struggles or are too complex to do anything about it. We begin with these questions in mind and by presenting two key paradoxes that will be at the center of our debate about whether our schools are maximizing the potential of all children in preparing them for a prosperous, new generation. We will call the first one the Dream-Reality Paradox and the second the Price-of-One Paradox.

In exploring these riddles, we will discover that our vision of full systems integration is already in place every day in every school system everywhere, and yet not in place at the same time. We will find that our school systems are designed with children in mind, but not with their success as our sole outcome. We will discover that our school systems are working exactly as they are designed, though not working very well for many, many children.

We will uncover that our systems are well intentioned and that we have no shortage of caring, dedicated educators and leaders. Still, we will debate whether any system that works for some but not others is a system at all, and we will question whether a school where some kids learn and others do not meets the truest definition for being a school. Yes, in honor of schools and children everywhere, honest answers will demand tough questions.

SCHOOL SYSTEMS ARE NOT ACTUALLY SYSTEMS

If we are ever to form the robust school systems that our kids deserve, the questions we explore should challenge our basic beliefs and definitions as educators and leaders. To get us started, let us endeavor to imagine, or even seek out personally if you wish, any leader in any school system anywhere. Then, let us ask if these leaders have an organized, aligned plan of attack for making our schools better, a system in place for positive change in their organizations. Let us ask them if their system already is, or is at least designed to be, a seamless dedication of people and processes, strategies, and interventions to make learning better for all children.

They will almost certainly say yes, and they are oftentimes wrong.

This is not to suggest that our leaders are not caring or well-informed. In fact, we have all had the great privilege of working with brilliant and talented people in the field. Across all school districts, we have confided in and commiserated with scores of accomplished leaders, from innovative teachers to inspiring school district superintendents. They are heroes all.

Without exception, they believe in the possibilities of public schooling, they care about children, they seek to improve their own practice, they are open to new ideas, and they are convinced we are moving in the right direction. Among all professionals everywhere, educators may be the most optimistic of all. They will complain and tell you that the system is broken, but they will also tell you that better days lie ahead. They are true believers.

Still, though good intentions are plentiful, successes are thin. Across our industry, we have not found consistent solutions to ensure learning for all children. We have not successfully engaged all children, many of whom still tell us that school is rote and uninteresting. Within our most challenging schools, we have not found consistent strategies or efficient systems that provide surefire and lasting improvement. To be certain, our schools could be so much more.

As a result, there is still a great bit of sniping in our school districts from students, teachers, and leaders born out of a recurring frustration that our plans of attack are either futile against systems that are too large or too bureaucratic, or maddening and inefficient in their inability to affect real and lasting change.

In fact, of all the school systems in all the world, it is hard to find one that is everything it can be in terms of full systems integration to support learning for all children, including the boys and girls in the back rows. It is nearly impossible to find just the right interplay of people, departments, programs, and policies designed to improve schools and student mastery of standards in any consistent and lasting way. Still, we keep searching.

In schools and districts both large and small, ideas are played out over and over, and a roulette of solutions come and go. The money and related resources commissioned to impact change (from reading improvement to family involvement) are rarely consistent with sound, reliable returns on investment. Though each of us can point to a teacher, school, or department that is outshining the rest, there is scant evidence to point to the system as the agent for that success. In fact, pointing to "pockets of excellence" in a school or school district is not the definition of excellence at all. It is the definition of luck.

The Dream-Reality Paradox

The struggle to define our success, to agree on a well-designed plan of attack, and to resolve the gross misunderstandings and mischaracterizations of our work are at the heart of what we will call the Dream-Reality Paradox. This paradox is fashioned from the concerns of frustrated educators everywhere who have worked in schools for many, many years and from a lifetime of studies around systems change in school districts around the globe. Evidence of this troubling paradox is voiced nearly every day by nearly every school and district leader everywhere. They just don't know what to call it.

The conversation goes something like this:

Q: Do you believe that you have a good plan in place for change in your school or district?

A: Yes. Of course. Absolutely.

Q: If so, then why have you not seen dramatic and lasting improvement in your school(s)?

A: Well, we're not sure yet, but we're studying it. We're forming a committee and putting a new plan in place that we are certain will work this time. Trust me, we're close. Improvement is just around the corner.

This conversation is not presented to criticize or make light of the important role that positivity, planning, and strategizing play in creating lasting improvement. In fact, too much is at stake to simply poke fun at our solutions even when they come up short. (It is probably important to note here that any attempt to make fun at anyone is akin to making fun of myself, for I have spent a lifetime working in our schools and have experienced every type of success and failure that there is. Like you, I am the system. I represent both what is wrong with our current thinking and potentially what is right.) Yes, educators are paradoxes as well.

To fully understand this problem of practice that we are calling the Dream-Reality Paradox, let us restate the above conversation in a bit more detail:

Is your school system connected and aligned to improve learning?

- *Yes, the system is absolutely connected and aligned* (the Dream Paradox). It is interconnected through common vision statements, missions, goals, and action steps. The people and departments are in place to carry out those actions. A reporting structure is clearly articulated to provide suffi-

cient monitoring, support, and accountability. There is a general sense that the team is on the same page, and we have a strategic plan to prove it.
- *No, the system is not at all connected nor aligned* (the Reality Paradox). Though there are common goals and expectations, the people and departments work to large degrees in silos and serve their own purposes (the reading department works on reading; the math department works on math; the family engagement team works on increasing family engagement). The reporting structure is not designed to increase cross-departmental relationships and partnerships, nor does it foster common definitions and solutions among our teams. The system functions as a collection of parts without a whole, without a soul.

The painful truth about these two related and all-too-familiar descriptions of systems is that they are both correct. The system is almost always connected and not connected at the same time. And so begins a complex recipe for an elixir that provides leaders with an enduring confidence that things are going well while also stirring up a quiet resentment that the system is creeping toward mutually assured destruction. To understand how this plays out in our school systems, let us look at each slice of the paradox separately.

The Dream Paradox

No school or school system strategizes to fail. We have all been part of countless strategy sessions around how to make our school or district systems more streamlined and connected to learning. Those meetings are sometimes productive and always well meaning. Unlike other industries, school systems are pretty consistent regarding their outcomes. Our leaders want to improve reading and math achievement, increase graduation rates, and establish high expectations for all students so they graduate ready to tackle anything that life brings their way.

In presenting the Dream Paradox, we can say without hesitation that schools and school districts are designed to support learning. They have an organizational structure in place that is aligned to the work (see any organizational chart). They have sound strategies for improvement (see any strategic plan). They even have accountability measures and periodic checks on the system. When we stand back and look at it, everything appears to be what we envisioned. Yet, when the results come in, we have little to show for it. Alas, the system dreams big but awakens small.

The good news is that the system does dream, and the dreams of leaders are always the same. They dream success. All good leaders dream success. They can see it, some better than others, of course. They can draw it for you on a cocktail napkin or whiteboard, ramble on about it at a company social, or paint it for you with great eloquence at a district visioning retreat. Putting that dream to paper is hard, and strategizing for its success is even harder.

Even when those dreams become plans, and even when those plans become actions, the actions are often carried out by people who exist in a bureaucracy of endless hallways and email chains, meetings upon meetings, and budget constraints that provide many obstacles to success. This leads us to an unfortunate reality that is presented next.

The Reality Paradox

Even visionary leaders fail. It would be easier to say otherwise, but we all know of top-notch thinkers and dreamers who can articulate a vision and yet not see it through to success. We can all find top-notch strategists who put strong plans to paper only to see them come up short. If we have learned anything from the research around leadership and management, we know that there are many styles and methods of leading and that none of them paves a certain route to success.

The same can be said for systems themselves. A visionary, forward-thinking company can fail, as can a thoughtful, strategic company with what appears to be a sound business plan. If this were not so, then all companies would follow the same, surefire business model. The question about why some companies fail and some succeed is the basis for many, many books (this one notwithstanding). While this text does not dare to untangle the endless snarls of that question, it will serve as an on-ramp for school and district leaders in finding common definitions and solutions in solving the paradoxes presented above.

In doing so, we will find that no matter our management styles, objectives, experiences, and intentions, the system itself is to blame for the failures it faces. The system itself is too naïve or too proud to recognize the forces that are undermining its effectiveness, or it is too stubborn to fix them. In her delightful primer on systems development titled *Thinking in Systems*, Donella Meadows (2008) compares the frailties and failures of any system to the flu.

In the simplest terms, she points out that the flu bug isn't the only thing we can blame when we get sick. The flu itself isn't *solely* responsible for attacking the individual, for the individual is also to blame. We too are to blame for getting the flu, insomuch as we have not taken care of ourselves, gotten enough rest, or taken enough vitamins. We are the ones who set up the conditions by which we are attacked by the flu bug.

Worse than that, we might say that we are the sole cause of the flu by allowing ourselves to become sick in the first place. Meadows adroitly reminds us that any system that is not well-designed nor well-orchestrated from the start is destined to catch the flu and fail. "The system, to a large extent, causes its own behavior" (Meadows, 2008, p. 2).

When this happens, the unbecoming reality is that a looks-good-on-paper organizational structure (the dream) might provide us with a less-than-we-hoped-for outcome (the reality). Yes, one could argue that the cause of our failures might be blamed on outside forces, but our shortcomings are more likely the result of our internal decisions. The conditions for system success were just not there, despite our best intentions. Worse still, the conditions we established for success might have actually contributed to the poor outcomes. Why? Because the system didn't just wake up one day and catch the flu. It is far more likely that the system's ideas, for far too long, were tired, run down, and worn out. And that always leads to illness.

FLU REMEDIES/SOLVING THE RIDDLE

So why does this Dream *big/sad* Reality paradox occur? For one reason, schools and school districts are complex, nonlinear systems, and yet we keep looking for simple, linear solutions to our problems. Meadows (2008) describes the relationships as such:

- *A linear relationship* is one that exists between two elements in a system and can be drawn on a graph with a straight line. It is a relationship with constant proportions.
- *A nonlinear relationship* is one in which the cause does not produce a proportional effect. The relationship between cause and effect can only be drawn with curves and wiggles, not a straight line. (p. 91)

To be clear, schools and school districts too often believe that there is a straight line between problems and solutions. We have all seen a school's math scores drop and heard someone speak up and say: "Let's provide them a math coach." Even though a math coach could help, the entire solution supposes that poor math instruction is the root cause at the school, that we have a strong math coach to hire, or that the teachers are open to coaching to begin with.

Any attempt to create simple, direct solutions within complex systems is certain to fail unless those solutions are aligned to related solutions in an endless web of training, supports, and actions that are interconnected and interdependent. Anything less and we are not functioning as a system. Instead, we are functioning as a bureaucracy. Though some students thrive within our bureaucracies, many do not. One reason for this is obvious to anyone who has worked in a school system. We have so much stuff going on and so many people to manage it that we cannot focus. We simply cannot get out of our own ways.

Mark Twain said it best when he remarked that education is "what you must acquire without any interference from your schooling." If we were honest about our work and the results we are getting, we would admit that, despite our best intentions, our efforts might actually be inhibiting student learning. If we were honest, we would admit that a robust educational system designed to educate all children at the highest cognitive levels would look much, much different than the one we have now.

THE ECOLOGY OF HONEST-TO-GOD SYSTEMS

There has been so much talk for so many years about the need for school systems to improve their alignment of people and processes that most of us are left to wonder what we are missing, as our leaders step forward to repurpose one familiar idea after another. The sentiment that "Haven't we seen this before?" is pervasive throughout education because we have all been in the classroom or boardroom together many, many times (even recently, I assume).

We've all been there amid another round of strategy meetings designed to produce a round of draft plans and organizational charts that have us all wondering what good all this systems talk has done us if we are not any more aligned than we were ten or twenty years ago. Worse yet, we may find that we are not even aligned in our definition of what an aligned system is, let alone in agreement on the preferred outcomes, or how to measure our progress along the way.

Meadows (2008) provides us with a succinct definition of systems and, in doing so, provides additional context for tackling our conundrum. She describes a system as "a set of things—people, cells, molecules or whatever—interconnected in such a way that they produce their own pattern of behavior over time" (p. 2). Knowing what we know of schools and school districts, let us start with this definition in connecting our systems vision to the realities we face in education. While this is a fine definition, it does not mesh with what we know of school systems, and it begs the further unraveling of the yarns we weave through our paradoxes.

You see, systems thinkers would have us ask ourselves if the systems we have are "interconnected" and whether these interconnected things (people or departments in our industry) produce "patterns of behavior." If that is our working definition, then we have a long way to go before we can call our schools and school system a "system."

While no one working in a school district today would suggest that we have not mastered the art of producing "patterns of behavior" (which may be too many to count), one would have to question whether those patterns are the result of our interconnections (which, sadly, may be too few to name). Moreover, we might have to question whether some of the patterns of behavior we are producing in terms of student outcomes and teacher practice are the exact opposite of what we wish for.

Of course, all of this depends on who is buying the notion that school districts are systems in the first place or if we accept the characterization of systems as interconnected and, in turn, productive and meaningful. While even a glass-half-empty observer of a school system would suggest that there are certainly patterns and processes in place, the glass-half-full observer would have to conclude that those patterns are not always producing positive gains and (even if they are) they are more likely to feel more like ruts than routines, more encumbering than empowering. Alas, our conundrum remains.

While this can be frustrating, the good news is that the leaders of our school systems have a great opportunity and responsibility to fix it. As with any great challenge, this is where leadership steps in. It was Mahatma Gandhi who challenged us to "be the change we wish to see in this world." You see, Gandhi would never blame the system for the system's ills. He would blame the leaders who birthed and nurtured the system and who are much more responsible for its woes than the system itself.

Systems theorist and author Peter Senge (1990) tells it this way: "We tend to blame outside circumstances for our problems. 'Someone else'—the competitors, the press, the changing mood of the marketplace, the government—did it to us. Systems thinking shows us that there is no outside; that you and the cause of your problems are part of a single system. The cure lies in your relationship with your 'enemy'" (p. 67).

Whether good or bad, the enemies of our school systems are found within. Uncovering and battling these foes will not be easy and will require our next generation of leaders to create new and better systems than the ones we have now. Whatever they look like, our students and parents will demand that they be systems of character, integrity, and innovation that are built from an instructional core that is so strong and unmistakable that everything we do breathes life from it.

No matter what these systems look like, they will be living systems that are rooted in student learning outcomes and carried out with such high degrees of alignment and efficiency that no actions can be taken that do not positively impact children and their futures.

LESSONS FOUND IN OTHER SYSTEMS/MODELS FOR CHANGE

In search of solutions that will push us in new and creative ways, it is critical that we look outside our own industry for answers and beyond the management texts we pour over in search of any morsel that we're still missing. This quest for fresh ideas will require us to explore a richer understanding of what we mean by "systems" and a deeper appreciation of what mature systems are (or can be). It will be equally critical that we are honest about the outcomes (sometimes trivial and often serious) that result from our shared misunderstandings of systems or misapplication of systems thinking.

As we sift through all these systems "what if" and "what fors," let us begin our exploration by paying homage to one of our generation's most compelling scientists, philosophers, and social architects, Austrian-American physicist Fritjof Capra. (I can still recall the day when I discovered his wonderful exegesis *The Tao of Physics* while on a camping trip with my wife, just the two of us . . . three counting Capra.)

Capra is one of many muses from the fields of systems ecology, physics, and philosophy who have much to offer us as educators and innovators. Though there are too many of these experts to name here, some of them are quoted throughout this book; others remain unnamed, but they inspired this text nonetheless. As we encounter deep thinkers like Capra and others, it is important to remind ourselves that each one of us is set upon a life mission that is probably much alike among us.

Most of us are seeking rich connections among our work and lives, among the successes and failures we are experiencing, among the flowering prose and torched rhetoric we are hearing from poets, prophets, and politicians, and even among the deep questions we all have around science, religion, and faith. These are the connections and deeper meanings that we all seek while we drift away, deep in thought, on lonely afternoons (sometimes with a glass of wine in hand and sometimes with two).

To best prepare us for what these systems intellectuals have to tell us, let us consider what arises during those quiet moments of deep intellectualism and meditation that we all share. Let us consider what we all picture when we are alone, there in our quiet places. What do we envision our lives to be? What do we wish our schools to be?

In those moments, most of us admit that there is a larger something that we all seek to uncover, a greater "whole" that is quite hard to grasp, a grander purpose in play that we do not see while we are at our workplaces racing between hallways, trying to make it to Friday, tinkering with new solutions, opening up a new box of strategies, reading and re-reading the directions, and meddling in the minutiae.

In these moments of deep meditation, most of us see the very same things. We picture the possibilities of an educational system where everything is working as planned. We see all children and all teachers succeeding. We see them engaged, inspired, and confident. We see them smiling. In those moments, we do not see budgets or departments or strategies.

In fact, it is fair to say that the larger purpose of our educational system, the bold experiment that we call public education and its grand promise to educate all children everywhere, is the same vision that we all share in the end. If we can agree on that much, then we might describe our common vision of what our school systems could be as the "whole" and the people, departments, plans, and processes as simply the "parts" we have in place to get us there.

If you will, imagine then a school system that is so aligned, that is so tightly fixed on creating a perfect, seamless whole, that we no longer see the parts at all. In fact, this is a good time to remind us that it was Aristotle who offered us his prescient theory that the "the whole is greater than the sum of its parts."

This daring hypothesis that everything is connected to everything else (and serves a greater purpose) may be new to some educators but is not new to scientists and intellectuals across many, many disciplines. In fact, it is increasingly common to find the hard sciences of biology, physics, and others reaching very similar conclusions to those proclaimed by Aristotle and others.

Many scientists are now toggling back and forth between making meaning of things in purely scientific manners and exploring those loose affiliations that science simply cannot deny nor explain away. We can view those connections and purposes as something spiritual or something natural. Either way, even the best attempts by our scientists to break everything down into smaller and smaller parts has led to more evidence that all things everywhere, in the end, are intertwined and symbiotic.

Though mixing science and religion creates a messy batter indeed, we will delve into these matters at a surface level as a way of framing our pursuit of fully functioning systems. For those who struggle with the term *religion*, let us agree to define any unexplained phenomena as "spiritual." Still, it is fair to posit that any honest attempt to find purpose in our work as school leaders leads us into the same discussions that scientists are having about countless other systems among us, both simple and complex. Our colleagues across many disciplines are asking important questions like:

- What is the impact of a particular action versus another?
- How might those actions impact intended and unintended outcomes?
- How closely are our actions, people, and processes aligned?
- What is the nature of change, and in turn, what is the nature of things we cannot explain?

Capra is one among many who has spent a lifetime spreading the gospel of systems theory and challenging the scientific community to consider the connections and nuances that are only found among the ecologies of living systems. In his brave attempt to present physics as the new model for all sciences, Capra delved deep into the science of microorganisms. Like many scientists, he was convinced that he would find the meaning of things among his study of the smallest of very small things.

Along the way, he discovered something that he never thought he would. He found that most things in the world cannot be adequately separated, sorted, and categorized because those things are all connected and alive, more spiritual in their makeup than a science like physics could hope to explain. While we can always describe and marvel at the whole thing (big things), we cannot find nor make sense of the parts (the little things). Capra (1996) called this the "basic tension" between the parts and the whole (p. 17).

What Capra uncovered was that the indescribable beauty of living things (systems) is so intertwined and so sublime that there was no use parceling out the microtendencies that nourished its existence. His attempt to isolate the parts was futile because the parts were drawing their energy from the system itself. The whole gave life to the parts, not the other way around.

Senge has found similar patterns among organizations. He declares that we cannot separate one department's success from another's. That no matter our individual roles or plans or actions, we each impact the whole system. What this means for us as leaders is that we are both the problem and the solutions to the changes that we seek. "To understand the most challenging managerial issues requires seeing the whole system that generates the issues" (Senge, 1990, p. 66).

DEVELOPING AN INSTRUCTIONAL SOUL/LEARNING AS A CORE VALUE

Extant research findings portend a universal truth that the system cannot be viewed by its parts and pieces and that our frustrations around the slow rate of progress in our schools is both one of our own making and immediately fixable. Of course, designing an alluring new system will first require us to envision how beautiful it could someday be. And now we're finally getting somewhere. Because designing the robust school system that we all envision will require us to fully define and not stray from the rich, instructional outcomes that we seek.

In their book *Strategy in Action*, Rachel Curtis and Elizabeth City (2015) make a compelling case that everything we do in schools must center on learning and the people who carry out those learning initiatives. Yes, this may be obvious, but it is much easier said than done. This is especially difficult in light of the departmentalization and bureaucracy that disconnects people from the larger mission of student learning.

Any study of systems will provide evidence that it is possible to design departments and actions that are aligned to each other and to common values that connect people and practices. In turn, these types of systems establish more desirable schools and workplaces that are focused on human conditions, not bureaucratic ones.

The science of ecology is an appropriate discipline to describe these robust systems because it involves the interactions of living things (organisms) to other living things, a highly complex recipe of relationships and meanings. We would all do well to study this research more. To this end, a more complete summary of this fascinating discipline and its implications for our work is found in chapter 7. In short, the world's ecologies are so complex that science has created manageable frameworks for us to better understand their constructs.

To give us a taste of this, let us review an example that we all recognize from the science of biology. This familiar discipline is organized into nested hierarchies ranging from genes, cells, and tissues on up to a larger biosphere. Together, hierarchies form a panarchy, an integrative framework that seeks to account for the complex interactions and characteristics of systems, including ecological, economic, and social models.

Without getting too technical, this panarchy unveils a hard-to-imagine certainty of nonlinear behaviors, which means that the connections, causes, and effects we find are not always proportionate and (pay attention here) that small changes to critical variables can lead to disproportionate, even dramatic changes to the overall system properties, perhaps even some that are irreversible.

Yes, we have biology to thank for the science of ecology and for introducing us to new terms like *network* and *community*. Of course, scientists now tell us that the study of communities only leads to more communities embedded inside those (picture one of those Russian nesting dolls), leaving us to wonder where it all ends.

So what does all this science talk mean for our school and district leaders? As a start, it means that we must proceed with great caution when we consider fixing our schools and districts one subject, one crisis, or one department at a time. It means that we should be wary to note that the fixes we are putting into place may be affecting other fixes or, quite possibly, creating new crises that will require yet more solutions, plans, people, and processes later. Alas, we have made these mistakes before and, in doing so, have joined the panoply of thinkers and problem-solvers that have cautioned us against the inadequacies of fixing the parts with little or no consideration of what we are doing to the whole.

We can all recall staring in awe upon our first discovery of a natural wonder like Niagara Falls or the Grand Canyon. We are reminded in those moments that we need our eyes only for the purpose of seeing amazing things. Eyes have no other function, no independent role to play. It is even fair to say that the reason we seek to care for and protect our eyes is not for the sake of our eyes, per se, but only to preserve the beauty that seeing provides us.

What does this mean to us as systems thinkers? It means that we should focus less on protecting our eyes and more on making the things we see beautiful. Because there is no reason to see if there is nothing worth looking at, that to be blind is not such a terrible thing as a lack of seeing is. Again, we will explore this complex reality further in the chapters that follow.

THE MAP IS NOT THE TERRITORY: A LESSON IN STRATEGIC PLANNING

As systems leaders, the great task in front of us is to make the task of systems change not so great because of us. As we develop more vibrant, engaging, and impactful school systems, we will need to find ways to create simple plans and not stray from them. Then we will have to create systems of mutual accountability to ensure that we wake up in the morning and are certain that the actions we agreed upon are carried out relentlessly.

Along the way, we must resist, at all costs, rewriting our plans over and over again or attacking the progress measures we have in place as being inadequate. Why? Because we cannot just change the needle out every time we fail to move it. Because learning outcomes are the only things that matter. Because the success of boys and girls like those in the back of the classroom are the only things we seek. Because the plan we put into place is not the solution, and the system is not the solution. Only the solution is the solution. Let's return to Capra (2000 [1975]) to unpack this for us:

> For most of us it is very difficult to be constantly aware of the limitations and of the relativity of conceptual knowledge. Because our representation of reality is so much easier to grasp than reality itself, we tend to confuse the two and to take our concepts and symbols for reality. It is one of the main aims of Eastern mysticism to rid us of this confusion. Zen Buddhists say that a finger is needed to point at the moon, but that we should not trouble ourselves with the finger once the moon is recognized; the Taoist sage Chuang Tzu wrote: "Fishing baskets are employed to catch fish; but when the fish are got, the men forget the baskets; snares are employed to catch hares; but when the hares are got, men forget the snares. Words are employed to convey idea; but when the ideas are grasped, men forget the words." In the west, the semanticist Alfred Korzybski made exactly the same point with his powerful slogan, "The map is not the territory." (p. 28)

To stretch our thinking a bit, we might say that our ultimate plan is to no longer need a plan. For when the plan provides us with results, the victory comes when we toss out the plan and embrace the reality of our newfound success. To help us visualize this a bit better, think of it like a silly tradition that some may be familiar with. Across some communities or families, it remains an annual rite of passage for the kids to empty out their backpacks at the end of a school year, to gather up the year's homework assignments, essays, and tattered notebooks and (wait for it) toss them in a bonfire.

This is probably not something that one should admit among teachers and principals, so please forgive this small transgression. Still, the notion that homework is simply a means to an end is the point of the children's celebration. This is not to suggest that homework isn't valuable (because it sometimes is); it is just that the homework assignments and notebooks were only important for a short time along each child's journey to mastery. Yes, it is quite important to celebrate the journey. Still, it is just as important to know that the journey is not the destination. The map is not the territory.

Of course, no one is suggesting that we don't need strategic plans, only that our plans are often too broad and random to affect real change, and that we are sometimes fixated on the plans themselves and less on the execution of them. It is evident across our industry that we are out of balance in spending too much time writing plans, revising them, and measuring our progress, and too little time acting on those good intentions. This is a common reality we call "paralyzed by process," and it's a symptom of a disease of rhetoric and red tape that we call "bureaucracy."

BUREAUCRACIES MASKED AS SYSTEMS

The future of our school systems will require us to not lose sight of the fact that plans are not solutions. Though planning is absolutely critical, it is best that we describe a strong, strategic plan as only an outline or blueprint for the solution itself. Whatever distinctions we make, a word of caution is in order here for our leaders. We must be careful to know that any plan that goes unchecked, no matter how well-designed, can grow into something so unwieldy that it can actually hinder growth.

We see this all the time in education, in large part because plans require people to execute them, and those people require even more people to check up on them, and those people need budgets, secretaries, and corner offices. Of course, we need mechanisms for measuring the plan's growth and communication plans to celebrate their successes. And, certainly, everybody involved needs a retirement plan and two weeks of paid vacation.

You see the point. Suddenly, the plan has grown into something that we hardly recognize, and the plan isn't about solutions anymore. The plan is only about keeping the plan alive, so all those people can stay employed and write more plans. This is a key point if we are to resolve our debate about whether our school systems are operating as systems or not. While some of us may be convinced that these people and processes represent a *system* for improvement and that most things are strongly aligned, others might accurately term all of this a *bureaucracy*. Across many industries, what most are calling "systems" are more likely bureaucracies masked as systems.

While it is easy to pick on such things (see Congress), there are some benefits to organized bureaucracies, from organizational charts to checks and balances. In fact, there was a time when schools were not assembled under centralized district leadership, though the pressure to find common curricula, standards, and accountability metrics changed all of that. The growing number of students influenced the implementation of a bureaucratic system. There were just too many of them to have a decentralized method of education (Kliebard, 2004).

Towns and villages could not manage the large number of students entering their schools, and bureaucracy was an appealing method of structuring the educational system from the perspective of the administrator. There were also pressures from industry to produce workers who were skilled in the tasks required by the modern workplace. To produce the most efficient workers, schools had to implement a systematic method of assessment that included written examinations of the students as a measurement of their skills.

Sadly, what was lost almost immediately in all of this measuring, sorting, and efficiency was the soul of the system itself. Educational historian Herbert Kliebard (2004) describes this decline in his book *The Struggle for the American Curriculum*. He writes: "As cities grew, the schools were no longer the direct instruments of a visible and unified community." Instead, schools were viewed as institutions where "norms and ways of surviving the new industrial society would be conveyed" (p. 1).

Our schools no longer had an authentic, tangible presence. Schools were no longer what Kliebard called the "centers of gravity" for their communities, and they have never regained this preferred status since. Somewhere in the move to centralized systems, we lost sight of the big picture. We lost sight of the uniqueness of the individual child. Suddenly, we were less personal, less creative. We were soulless.

SYSTEMS AS CENTERS OF GRAVITY

Regaining our souls will not be easy. It will require that we wrestle with the possibility that these robust systems we all imagine and want are even more complex and nuanced than any department strategy could dare to impact. It will require us to question if the departments we work in are designed to serve the system (the whole) or designed to serve themselves (the parts). Along the way, we might find that these things we call "departments" or "divisions" or even "subjects" are not systems at all but are put into place for our own sense-making, so we can sort out what the heck we are doing.

This means that one of our greatest challenges as school and district leaders will be changing our mindsets, as we are so entrenched in the bureaucracy that we know that it will be hard for us to imagine another way. Whatever we decide, we will not mold our next generation schools as centers of gravity by simply stoking the same old bureaucracy.

The upcoming chapters will challenge us to refire and rebrand a new way of schooling that is highly gravitational. This new way of doing things will draw together our children, parents, teachers, and community leaders in a manner that is much more organic and less institutionalized than what we have now. Like any emerging idea, this one is a work in progress and builds on some successes that we already have in place. Like any emerging idea, this one will require pioneering leadership.

This brings us to back to the boy in the back row and to our final paradox. We will call it the Price-of-One Paradox. What is true for the boy in the back row is true for most students across all cultures and all schools. In truth, our schools, as presently designed, do not successfully educate everyone, nor do we graduate all children ready for college, career, and life. Why is this? Because the system, as presently designed, can afford to lose one child, or even two or three or four along the way.

In fact, we all celebrate our reading scores and graduation rates even if dozens and dozens of students each year do not make the cut. No matter the number of students we lose, the system toils on. There is no lasting harm to the system when it loses the boy or girl in the back row, for the system itself (like all systems) is designed first to keep the system alive, and the system itself (not the child) always, always comes first. This is not just true of school systems, but all systems.

The good news is that we have created the system and we can recreate it. We have the authority and capacity to do this if we empower and embolden a new generation of leaders who can reshape our schools and school districts, who can inspire our teachers and staffs to rally around the common goal of engaging and challenging all students, of graduating each and every one of them with high literacy and math skills, and with advanced social, emotional competencies.

If we are so bold, we can mold a vibrant system that gives the boys and girls in the back row a sense of purpose that even they matter, that even they can change the world.

Chapter Two

Discovering Our Souls

Most leaders across most school districts describe themselves as systems thinkers. In fact, most will tell you that strong systems are required to bring order and purpose to the chaotic world of education, providing the critical linkages that give efficiency and meaning to our work in schools. Those leaders would be right. In fact, at this point, you may insert your favorite systems metaphor here. A web. A wheel. Some concentric circles, maybe. Perhaps a giant arrow comprised of several smaller arrows, all pointed upward in an illustration of common purpose.

So why is it that all this talk of systems thinking, strategic planning, and vision statements doesn't always lead to stronger alignment, increased efficiency, or even greater camaraderie? Why it is that even when system leaders are "true-believers" and can articulate a clear sense of direction that there is too little to show for their efforts and no real translation to honest-to-God system improvements once everyone returns to their offices, cubicles, and classrooms?

These questions presume, of course, that the systems conversations in schools and school districts are built from a common set of principles, a shared agreement on a few meaningful and measurable inputs and outcomes, and a series of aligned resources to get us there. The questions also posit that there exists a solid center from which an umbilical system is created, an array of departments and divisions, plans and processes that are connected to a core that brings common sense to our decisions and order to chaos. The questions above bring us back to the riddle presented in chapter 1: what appears on paper to be is a system is not a system at all.

To continue our dissection of this conundrum, let us zoom in a bit. Actually, let's zoom in *a lot*. Closer. Closer. Closer. Let us look behind the organizational charts and vision statements. Let us peel back the rhetoric and action plans to see what is behind all this strategy and policy talk. As we do, what we may find is that there is no *there* there.

What we may find is a void somewhere deep below the surface, the absence of a true center, a nucleus, a core. In fact, what we might find in many schools and school districts is little unity of purpose and no well-defined set of core beliefs that drives our decisions and links our plans, policies, and practices.

More than that, we may find that, even among those organizations that seem to have strong core values, those values may not be in sync with each other, drawing their collective energy from a common source, an absolute, everybody-on-the-same-page, no-doubt-about-it instructional center from which all our decisions gain life and meaning.

A soul.

To deepen our understanding of this instructional soul, let us shift our mental models for a moment from system webs and wheels to something described in more human terms. Let us close our eyes a minute and imagine more profound examples of systems in motion. If we do, we might envision a rugby scrum, arms locked so tightly that you can't tell where one man starts and another one ends, heads down in singular focus, all eyes on the ball, legs moving with common purpose. Each player's sweat and toil comingling and each man critical to winning the day.

Or we might imagine something else, like soldiers standing adroitly in pursuit of common victory, marching with youthful exuberance along narrow roads in a distant land. We might picture them in World War II attire, so famously etched in our memories from grainy black-and-white images, with liberation in their sights and resolve in their hearts. Or we might close our eyes and recall a tableau of weathered faces marching as one in the 1960s, arms swaying in unison along a rusty bridge in Selma, Alabama, or along a thousand other well-worn paths. In fact, if we listen, we might even hear their faint cries of desperation and prayer.

> We shall overcome, we shall overcome,
> We shall overcome someday;
> Oh, deep in my heart, I do believe,
> We shall overcome someday....
> We are not afraid, we are not afraid,
> We are not afraid today;
> Oh, deep in my heart, I do believe,
> We are not afraid today.

Each of these visions provides for us a model of what is meant by systems with a soul. Though these illustrations may inspire our work in setting common purpose, none of them matches what we find in most schools today. Yes, educators do have big hearts and big ideas. Yes, we tend to say the right things. Still, a prevailing frustration rumbles across our schools if only we listened closely enough.

If we slowed down and moved in closer, we would hear a faint cry for more time, greater focus, deeper collaboration, and more meaningful dialogue in accomplishing much more in our schools than we do now. What we would hear is a common refrain of confusion and isolation across school systems everywhere. Once again, the system dreams big but awakens small.

The truth is, the turnstile of initiatives, standards, and accountability mandates has left many schools mired in bureaucracy and inefficiency. This is why it feels as if our teachers and principals are running down the escalator in hopes of catching the subway train, only to find it left the station long ago. They are left with little choice but to chase the train down the tunnel, tossing in its way more parts, more solutions, more accountability measures, and more people and policies in an endless spray of graffiti that to some may look like artwork but to most of us is institutional vandalism.

SOUL SEARCHING IN SCHOOLS TODAY

If we were ever to set upon an honest assessment of the progress we are making, we would begin by asking our teachers and students on the front lines. Though it is hard to admit sometimes, our district leaders (and even some principals) are simply too mired in the bureaucracy we've described to provide a subjective analysis. Even among thoughtful leaders, their self-assessment of progress tends to sound more like self-aggrandizement.

This is not lost on the boy in the back row. If we ask him, he will tell us that he does not see the connections nor the purpose in his schooling, even if the principal or district leader has it all spelled out in a brochure or strategic plan. In turn, the boy tunes out and becomes another statistic, along with thousands of boys and girls like him. This is not for a lack of caring, but for a lack of systems.

Though the words of most leaders are pointed and meaningful, they too must admit that our students are not wrong. Too many children across too many schools either do not graduate or leave us underprepared for college, career, and life. This is especially true for students from low-income families and for students of color. There is no other conclusion that can be reached.

Across our school districts, we have not found consistent solutions to ensure learning for all children, nor consistent strategies for school improvement, nor efficient systems to maximize teacher effectiveness. Though we can all point to a principal or school here or there as a model of effectiveness, we have many others that do not measure up. No matter the vision, charisma, and bombast of a district superintendent or the planning and prodding of a district supervisor, variance among schools and school leaders is great.

The good news is that tighter alignment and deeper purpose are very much possible, now more than ever. Across school districts everywhere, we see a growing number of dynamic, young teachers and leaders who are ready to pursue innovative instructional changes. Fascinating experiments in curriculum and instruction are underway in many, many schools.

In fact, let us be clear that we are making strong progress as an industry, if only we were bold enough to go all in. We have seen some measurable strides across our schools in the amount and degree of hands-on learning, student collaboration, personalization, agency, and voice, and that provides strong evidence that better days lie ahead.

In fact, if the ideas proposed in this book had been suggested ten or twenty years ago, they would have been laughed out of the room. Now, with so much research behind our work in the areas of systems theory, school turnaround, and teacher practice, the time is ripe to brave a robust, new educational model led by a new generation of inspiring leaders.

INSTRUCTIONAL SOUL: A WORKING DEFINITION

It should be noted first that the metaphor of a soul is not important to our cause, nor is its purpose as an acronym below. These are simply rhetorical devices used to qualify and synthesize our methodology for systems change. Across the wide landscape of public, private, and charter schools, there are many exciting school models being tested as we speak. In the end, it does not matter how we label any of these models, as long as they contain the following attributes.

Extant research findings tell us that if our solutions are to be effective and scalable, they must be student-centered and systematic. This means that if we are going to bear witness to sustainable change in our schools and richer learning experiences for our students, our solutions must include the following characteristics (see also figure 2.1):

- *(S) Systematic (aligned).* We must subscribe to a full-on, systems approach in our school districts to ensure alignment within and across our classrooms. Nothing we do can be random. We simply cannot afford it. We do not have the money, time, or patience even to implement solutions that are inefficient. Developing pockets of excellence in our school districts that are not scalable costs much too much for us to consider them as models for improvement. We must connect all initiatives, and not just in name but in action. This means that all departments, decisions, budgets, processes, plans, and measures must be aligned to impact learning at all costs.

- *(O) Organic (authentic)*. We must reinterpret our current standards, lessons, and outcomes to ensure that highly relevant learning experiences are the norm in our classrooms. We can no longer afford to view schooling and assessment through the narrow lens of the subjects that we teach, nor can we afford to view all disciplines and outcomes as equally important and mutually exclusive. They are not. Further, we must embrace the twenty-first-century skills (including soft skills) that the world demands and build cross-disciplinary curricula around those things (not around subjects). This can be accomplished via a rich array of authentic school and community experiences led by students and designed to grow their skills toward self-sufficiency and even self-actualization.
- *(U) Unified (relational)*. We must reorganize our structures to intentionally build richer relationships within our schools and across departments. This will require us to carry out actions designed to enrich and empower the lives of teachers and students, including a broader leadership structure that gives teachers and students much greater voice in decision-making. It will require us to build deeper bonds of trust, of mutual understanding, and of shared accountability. It will also demand honest dialogue about the barriers we have to learning, including race and poverty, parental responsibility, systems resistance, and staff buy-in. If we do this well, we will view each child as special and unique, and we will blame others less. We will subscribe to a brave, new notion that losing even one child to poverty, gangs, drugs, or dropping out is disastrous for the entire community, not just for the child and his or her family.
- *(L) Learner-centered (personalized)*. We must view all decisions through a learning lens, and not as operational or transactional maneuvers. Across schools and district offices, nothing is worth doing that doesn't lead directly to learning outcomes for every child. Every department and every person must be working to improve students' academic and social-emotional skills. The complaint that some students have deficits so great that the system cannot repair them is outmoded. The notion that some students with certain life advantages will outperform others is antiquated and unacceptable. The idea that a child's ability to master a subject is dependent on how lucky he or she gets in securing a great teacher is not, in any way, a systems solution. Leaders must design systems in which each and every educator, parent, and community agency impacts student learning in deliberate and cross-functional ways. This will demand that each and every one of us are experts in teaching and learning, and that all decisions are made in the best interests of learning for all.

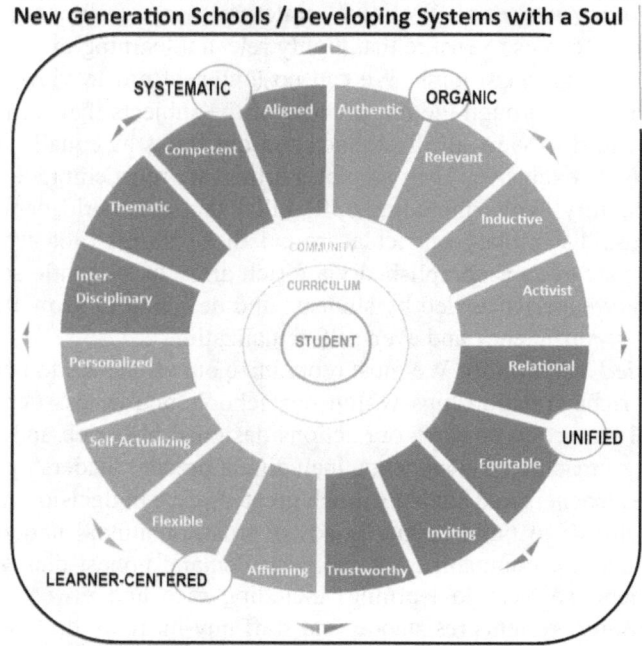

Figure 2.1. New Generation Schools/Developing Systems with a Soul

FROM TRANSACTIONAL LEADERSHIP TO SOULFUL LEADERSHIP

The change we seek in our schools must begin with our principals. No matter the good intentions of our district leaders, the heavy lift of school improvement has always been carried out differently across schools, with principals at the helm and with the lives of many, many children at stake. In fact, our school principals are so critical to our future as an industry that we must envision a new leadership model and fashion a bold leadership construct for supporting teachers and children.

As always, the principals we employ and the training they undergo will be key. This is not new thinking, for principals have always been at the center of school reform. While state and district leaders propose one tired solution after the next, school principals discover their own dynamic solutions for transforming their schools. We have learned much from great principals along the way, and the research is rich in best practices.

In fact, it should be noted that the systems revolution being proposed via this text may lead to much greater principal and school autonomy and a seismic shift away from the centralized school systems we have now. Our district leadership structures may also shift, from orchestrating change to facilitating it, from enabling principals and teachers to empowering them. This is another way of saying that school leaders must be the change they seek in their schools and must not look to the district or state to make their schools better. In truth, our best leaders never have.

As there is much research and many great books written about the actions and attributes of great principals, we will not reiterate those qualities here. Still, one has to wonder why we have not been successful yet in packaging those skills adequately as part of our professional development and why some principals have so much success while others cannot get out of their own way.

One thing we know for sure is that great principals can see a path to success in spite of the unending mandates and emails that clutter the road. They are uniquely confident and skilled at leading in deliberate, actionable ways that are designed to impact instructional improvement and student learning. Without a doubt, our best principals have something extra special, a unique ability to see things that others do not see, and to lead others in a manner that our current leadership trainings don't quite capture.

Our inability as an industry to transfer these innovative practices to all school leaders has left us void of consistent, reliable results and always yearning for a deeper bench. This is not a criticism of the many hardworking assistant principals and principals who are just trying to survive the day. They are leading their schools as they were trained to do. In fact, we have a long history of training our leaders to be operational in their thinking, to be transactional, to think inside the box, and to be safe. As a result, it is not unusual for our school leaders to be stifled by the system itself.

There are too many examples of principals who are told that their bold, new ideas should be put on hold because they are too expensive or too radical in upsetting the teacher's union, the parents, or the district superintendent. Yes, we talk a lot about vision and innovation, but those grand ideas are carried out by leaders who are conditioned otherwise.

REALITY CHECK: TOUGH QUESTIONS TO PONDER

Throughout our industry, we continue to learn from principals who challenge the status quo, who stare down the naysayers, and who are bold enough to zig when others zag. Our challenge then is to define and pinpoint exactly how these innovative principals go about their work that is different than the rest of us. In large part, capturing their skillsets is made more difficult because we are hard-pressed to find two schools (or two leaders) in any school district that are alike. That's a strange thing, really, since the research on best practices in school leadership have keyed on a few things that every school should do to increase learning.

In fact, most assistant principals and principals can recite these actions as if they were pilots readying for takeoff: increase the focus on standards—check; increase student engagement—check; increase time on-task—check; extend the school day—check; monitor classrooms through instructional rounds—check; make data-driven decisions—check; offer tiered interventions for students—check; flaps down, seats forward and in an upright position, cell phones off—check, check, check.

If only it were that easy. You see, there is something we are missing if all the school leaders in all the land are reading the same research and conducting the same book studies, and no two schools are going about this work in the same way. In fact, the variance in schools is so great that if our schools were college football teams, there may be just as many Alabamas and Clemsons in a school district as there are North Dakota States. Not only do our schools vary greatly in their makeup and mission, but also the leaders running those schools (and the district leaders advising them) often don't agree on what they should be doing and don't always define best practices in the same manner.

Even among leaders who have memorized the research and the jargon, they often struggle to reliably articulate the systems change they seek in any credible manner. This is one of the primary reasons why some schools are successful while others are not. There are too many fixes being proposed, too many interpretations of those solutions, too little time to implement them, too many mixed messages, and too little confidence that any of them will work.

In our frantic search for more solutions, we revisit the research, begin another book study, and offer more and more training, all in the hopes of finding the right nip and tuck to ensure a lovely figure, though finding too often that we have spent quite a lot of money and time putting lipstick on a pig.

For those who disagree, let us pose some tough questions. For those who suggest that their school district has it figured out, that they are much more evolved than the rest, let us pose even tougher questions. If all the principals in a school district (and all the teachers for that matter) attend the same district trainings, discuss and debate the same strategies, and follow and implement the same district plans, why do we see great variance across schools and classrooms?

Wouldn't we expect to find similar results if we have all attended the same trainings? Wouldn't a functioning system produce, at the very least, calibrated results across schools in terms of student outcomes, teacher performance, and leadership capacity? This is a good place to remind us that memorizing the company's mission statement doesn't make someone a missionary.

There are tough questions to ask if we are going to reengineer a better way to do schooling. For purposes of this book, we will only say that the variance we find across our schools is a symptom of systems dissonance. We will also propose that any variance in implementation would be greatly reduced if we successfully focused the expectations of our principals and teachers on a few key drivers of learning that are evidence based, reliable, and scalable.

If we did so, we would avoid the temptation to lead our schools in ways that feel more like fire drills, where there is so much noise that no one can hear, where everyone is scurrying about in search of the nearest exit, and where the point of it all is to leave everyone exhausted and frustrated in finding out that, by gosh, there was no fire to begin with. One obvious answer is daring a simpler and more dedicated approach to school improvement, one in which our leaders focus on doing a few things well. If done successfully, the synergy around school improvement would be real (not imagined) and the results might be lasting and profound.

A CALL TO ACTION: SCHOOL SYSTEMS FOR A NEW GENERATION

The next generation will bring great pressures on public schools to rebrand and repurpose their work. This will require leadership so bold and strides so daring that the resulting school structures will have those of us working in the industry now feeling as if we have landed in a *Back to the Future* movie. To avoid the cacophony of doomsday predictions we hear from uninformed media members and policy-makers, let us view this work as a challenge to evolve our systems faster and overcome the numbness that comes from sitting still too long.

Whether we embrace it or not, the future will require a more organic, soulful educational experience for our students that will not feel contrived and cookie cutter in having everybody follow the same bell schedule and complete the same assignments. If these changes do not occur, public schools could become the second choice (or last choice) of parents in the competitive market of schooling. If we are unable or unwilling to innovate, public schools will continue to exist but may become irrelevant in the marketplace.

To be clear about the degree of change being proposed, four key drivers (see figure 2.2) are described below that all leaders must consider if we are going to remain relevant for the next century. Each one will be explored throughout this text.

1. Revision school leadership
2. Restructure school systems
3. Repurpose school curriculum
4. Re-engage local communities

Revision School Leadership

The future will demand that we employ school principals and district leaders who are co-teachers, co-learners, and co-innovators alongside our teachers. This means that leaders must be experts in instruction because teachers will no longer follow leaders who are not great teachers themselves. Why? Because, in the next century, teachers will lead schools (not administrators). The shift will come. Yes, we will still need great leaders, but their work will shift from managers of people and policies to lead teachers, thought partners, and facilitators of teacher and student innovation.

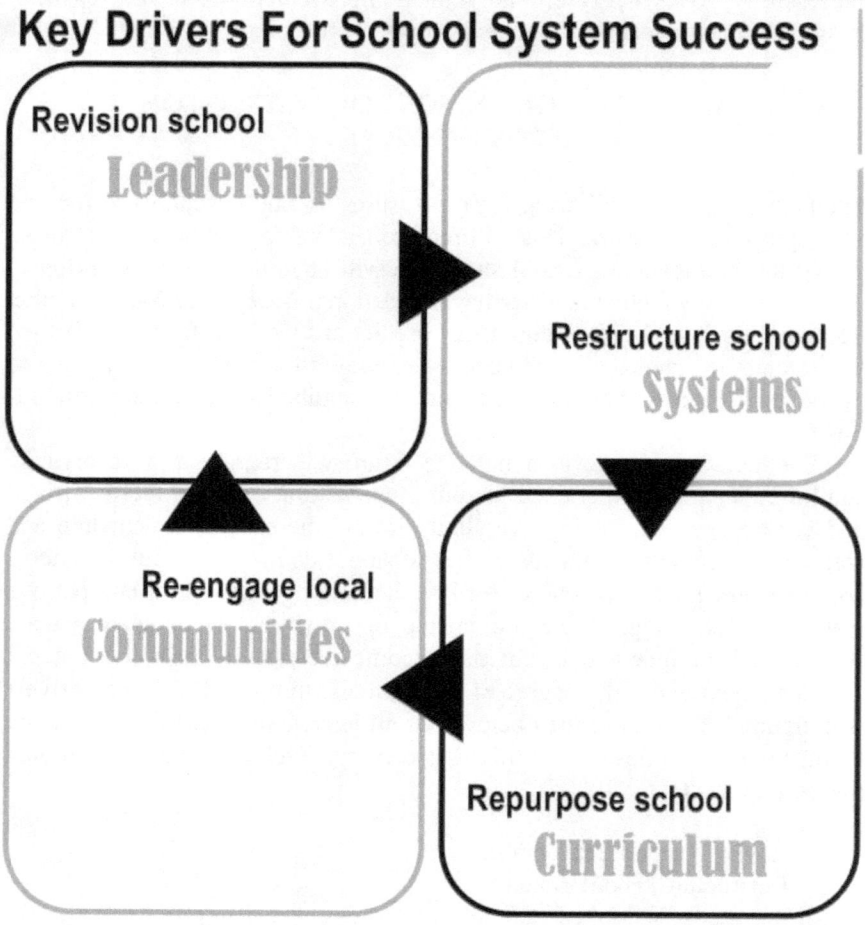

Figure 2.2. Key Drivers for School System Success

The next generation will demand that our leaders be inspirational, not operational. As mentioned, great principals continue to be the key agents for change, and that makes our selection of them hypercritical. The building manager is no more. Yes, operations will still be critical to student success, and someone will do that work. It just won't be the principal.

Restructure School Systems

The next evolution of schools and school systems will require us to reshape our district bureaucracies, from organizational charts and job descriptions to departmental goals and work products. This reorganization will be necessary to ensure greater efficiency around learning outcomes and fewer random arrows. It will demand that we flatten our organizational structures to become less vertical/hierarchical. At present, we don't just have too many chiefs; we have too many assistant chiefs, regional chiefs, and chiefs on special assignment.

This new type of district hierarchy might be described as a "parallel hierarchy" that is strongly aligned, highly perspicuous, and broadly accountable. It will demand that nearly every employee in every school and district office be held accountable for learning outcomes. The only exceptions will be those people who are expressly assigned to safety and security (bus drivers, security guards, campus monitors, deans, etc.). The system will have no use nor function for extraneous people who are not directly accountable for student learning. In fact, it won't even recognize them.

Repurpose School Curriculum

The future will demand a dramatic repurposing of our school curriculum, lessons, assessments, and outcomes. This change will arrive with such epic proportions that it will revolutionize the way we train, credential, and deploy our teaching forces. The tired structures, schedules, subjects, lessons, and tools we use now will feel like relics when this new era of schooling arrives. The rapid development of technology and our instant access to information will demand that our students be generalists (not specialists), activists, and problem-solvers.

To keep up, our curricula must be personalized and meaningful, even to the point that the assignments we work on in school directly improve the lives of our families and communities. Our students, parents, and business partners will demand that our schools be laboratories for innovation and leadership, social-emotional development, and creative expression. Not recitation. Not regurgitation. Nothing rote. Nothing routine.

Re-Engage Local Communities

The next century will forever connect our schools to their communities in such ways that our local parks, libraries, museums, and businesses will be our classrooms. Not sometimes (like on field trips), but all the time. The call for our curriculum and lessons to be highly relevant will only grow louder and student activism in their local communities will only grow stronger. In fact, there is a dramatic shift coming that most of us do not yet see. Our young people have become increasingly disinterested in our ancient hierarchies and outmoded credentialing that harken back to the industrial age. Our students are increasingly impatient, and that's not a bad thing.

They want to impact their communities right now. They want to engage in debate. They seek to be entrepreneurs in the present, with or without a formal education. Of course, some laugh at their unwillingness to wait their turns, as we did. In turn, they laugh at our willingness to tolerate such artificial barriers. By the way, that doesn't make them wrong. What this means for schools is that they must connect their lessons and activities to the real world, where kids live and work and engage in everything from video games and rap battles to local politics and church youth groups.

A PLACE TO START: CORE BELIEFS AND ACTIONS

If we are to be successful, this work must begin by strengthening our core. We must reach unwavering agreement on some key conditions for success, and ensure that all initiatives are derived from a few unyielding beliefs about how children learn. It seems only logical that we turn to our best teachers and leaders in drafting a blueprint for this change.

Among the lessons they have taught us are the following: They believe in children (high expectations). They are instructional experts (highly credible). They are focused, aligned, and intentional (highly systematic). They see things coming. They see things that others do not yet see. As such, they are able to narrow the scope of the work and make success manageable, personalized, and meaningful. They consider the consequences of their actions before they take any, and they plan accordingly.

Leaders like this are able to resist the allure of new ideas that the system is not yet ready for. They know when to say, "Why not? Let's go for it," and "Why now? Let's wait on that one." In turn, they are not distracted by the mirage that new things are needed when the solutions already in place might work if only given more time and attention. They know how to get from here to there with great efficiency.

If this is so, then we must consider whether these qualities and actions could be replicated in any school or school district. We might also wonder why they are not already. In fact, it should be noted that leading schools in deep and meaningful ways is possible for any leader in any system who is willing to buy into a few core beliefs, including those that some of us might support publicly but struggle with privately.

It doesn't matter what type of students we serve, for leading with an instructional soul is an approach that knows no race nor creed nor social status. It does not discriminate, whether you are fashioning in your mind an affluent, private school with only two hundred children or a large, urban public school with three thousand children. Still, it is not fair to propose substantive change without a substantive gut check for school and district leaders regarding the following beliefs:

- All children can learn. All children want to learn. *Children matter.*
- All parents want the best for their children. *Parents matter.*
- Teachers impact student learning. *Teachers matter.*
- School systems impact teacher effectiveness. *Systems matter.*
- Leaders impact system effectiveness. *Leaders matter.*
- All decisions are instructional decisions. *Decisions matter.*

These beliefs are well worth debating because instructional leadership requires some real soul-searching and some basic agreement on the above items before we can actually accomplish anything. In fact, the case can be made that these core beliefs are required antecedents for any lasting school improvement. This entire book, cover to cover, challenges the notion that these statements are untrue, disconnected, or even unnecessary for real change to occur.

LEADING SMALL/GETTING THINGS BACK INTO FOCUS

Lest we think that developing leaders and systems with a soul is so far removed from our current state that we might never get there, we should be clear that many leaders already operate in innovative ways that have set the groundwork for dramatic systems change. Though it may be hard to hear, it is in fact true that our most successful principals would be much further along in establishing a next-generation educational system if our state legislatures and district offices would get out of the way.

One of the things these principals know (out of necessity) is that they cannot implement too many solutions and expect them to be done with fidelity. They know that simple done well is always better than complexity half-assed. They also know that every decision they make each day either enhances or distracts from the learning targets they have set.

They know these things because our best principals are master practitioners, and they are also poets. They don't look at things like the rest of us do.

While we see trees and birds and flowers, poets see beauty and love and spirituality. They see meaning. They see connections. They hear music. Our best principals do as well, as they look out on the solutions they have put into place. They do as well.

Leaders with a soul see the purchase of new textbooks or computers as mechanisms for improving reading and math ability. The rest of us just "kind of" see that, and we miss the point entirely. We hear about a new lab of computers coming in, and we think first about how they might be used to test kids more efficiently. Then, we convince ourselves that testing kids more efficiently is tied to learning, though there are a series of subtle and important differences between these two viewpoints. One view has us focused on testing kids (even if we do so efficiently). The other view is focused on teaching them.

Of course, in school systems, leaders can often miss such subtleties because focus is not our friend. Discovering our instructional soul and then building a few key strategies connected to it requires us to simplify and narrow, something we rarely do well in school districts. We might call this "leading small." Our best leaders and school districts do this well. Our most struggling ones do not.

For those who have never worked in schools, let's be clear that many leaders suffer from doing many things so-so instead of doing a few things well (though this malady is probably common in companies large and small). Let us return to systems prophet Peter Senge, who cautions us to avoid falling victim to the allure of bureaucracy and complexity by making our systems and solutions even clunkier than they are now:

> Systems thinking finds its greatest benefits in helping us distinguish high- from low-leverage changes in highly complex situations. In effect, the art of systems thinking lies in seeing through complexity to the underlying structures generating change. Systems thinking does not mean ignoring complexity. Rather, it means organizing complexity into a coherent story that illuminates the causes of problems and how they can be remedied in enduring ways. The increasing complexity of today's world leads many managers to assume that they lack information they need to act effectively. I would suggest that the fundamental "information problem" faced by managers is not too little information but too much information. What we most need are ways to know what is important and what is not important, what variables to focus on and which to pay less attention to—and we need ways to do this which can help groups or teams develop shared understanding. (Senge, 1990, p. 128)

The good news for school districts is that we all understand our mission, and that mission is to educate children. So, without adding any further complexity to our work, we must simply agree on how to make learning happen for all students. Not metaphorically, but actually. Not theoretically, but practically. Can all kids learn? Yes or no? If the answer is yes, then what would it really take to make that happen? The system must ask those questions and act on the answers in intentional ways, which seems like a good place to remind us all that teachers and school leaders exist to serve children, not to serve the system.

Our transformation of schools will include narrowing our focus and seeking out purposeful connections between people and processes, curriculum and outcomes. If we do, we will go a long way toward leading people in ways that help them find value in their work while ushering in a new social architecture of our own making. As was presented in the previous chapter, systems intellectuals tell us that we cannot separate our actions from our beliefs and values, even if we try to.

True systems change will require us to channel (and yes, narrow) these values into some actions that actually accomplish something. That is where the work comes in, because all this prattling on about change must somehow play out in an ensemble of actual solutions instead of the random caterwauling of initiatives that we have now. Instead of a mission statement that we can all recite, we must inspire an instructional score in which we are all lead actors, seasoned, on pitch, and genuinely harmonious.

PRACTICAL EXAMPLES FOR SCHOOL PRINCIPALS

In plotting an example of such leadership, let's turn to a middle school principal who received wide accolades for her school's work in implementing reading and math instruction, monitoring academic rigor, and tracking student data in a personalized manner. It was the kind of school that others were asked to visit when they wanted to see an example of instructional focus, of a true leader who had a plan conceived around doing a few things well. While the school gained notoriety for its dedicated work, results on state assessments were not as strong as one would think, and both the district leaders and the principal grew increasingly frustrated.

This went on for two or three years until the district sent signals that it was time for a change, and the principal left. Of course, as fate would have it, a few days after her departure, the state reading and math scores arrived to great fanfare. They were exceptional. The school ranked among the top schools in the state in student growth.

The principal was right all along, especially in keeping her focus all the way to the end. She led her school from a common, narrow set of beliefs and actions and never wavered. Yes, she led with an instructional soul, though no one knew what to call it. As a starting point, this principal knew what great instruction looked like, and she kept her teachers, students, and herself focused there. No one questioned her credibility as an instructional leader.

Secondly, she had a skinny, deliberate plan to impact her school built around strong, core instructional beliefs. She resisted the temptation to change and take on the next big thing or too many things. This is another example of soulful leadership. In the face of pressure, she eschewed the creative suggestions offered by visitors to her school that she might try this or that, even when the improvement she was seeking took longer than she hoped for. It was too bad she left her school because she was right. She was right all along.

We will keep this principal in mind as we explore some common instructional dilemmas facing leaders today. Like the other examples provided in this text, the ones below do not represent the most important struggles facing our schools, nor are they equally important or mutually exclusive. They are simply provided as typical, practical realities that school principals face each day in dissecting how and why they carry out key actions.

CASE IN POINT: READING/LITERACY

Key Dilemma

Let us begin with the most obvious and common struggle facing educators everywhere: teaching kids to read and write. In fact, let us all slow down a minute and let this sad reality sink deep into our bones. After all of our years of instructional practice, and all the research on literacy, and millions of teachers taking part in this struggle, we still face the uncomfortable truth that nearly half of all children in America are not fully literate by any state or national standard. Yes, we have missed the mark by a great measure.

For every child who is graduating as a deep thinker and critical reader, there is another who is barely fluent or carries a scant vocabulary. Blaming that student's failures on his family or the state legislature doesn't cut it. We have to own it. We have to own our shortcomings. (Note: As a former English teacher and reading specialist, I own it with you.)

We stand as teachers and leaders who have not yet solved this crisis of conscience and problem of practice. Even as the research supports key drivers like small group instruction and exposure to complex tasks, we have to admit that we still struggle to execute these strategies in any consistent fashion across a school or grade level. Again, if we all read the same research, why is it that our successes are sporadic and our implementation sparse?

The lack of continuity we experience is nothing more than a lack of systems. To put this another way, the lack of success across schools or grade levels is a result of the great variance in the quality of instruction and processes found in most places. We have to conclude then that the "pockets of success" we celebrate are derived, not from true systems change, but from good fortune in the forms of good hiring (or not), timely training (or not), strategic scheduling (or not), or an inspirational curricula (or not).

Key Actions

In schools with a soul, learning is never lucky. Our best principals have taught us that learning cannot be left to chance. Let's trot out an example from an elementary school. First, a principal who is leading with an instructional soul would own her own hiring and training. This is not to say that the district office doesn't have a role to play, but that our best principals leave nothing to chance. Hiring a quality workforce and improving their practice must be every principal's primary mission to impact learning.

The principal in such a school would search for the strongest teachers as positions open, but also be on constant lookout for teachers who have applied to her school or district even when she has no openings. She would reach out to and prescreen candidates continuously, build immediate relationships at deep professional (even personal) levels, and possibly construct her own talent recruitment team and materials. The same can be said for the recruitment, hiring, and training of paraprofessionals and even adult mentors. She would leave nothing to chance in securing the most talented team possible.

With great intentionality, a top-flight principal would place her teachers into the appropriate grade levels based on their strengths and build robust professional learning communities that foster shared trust and learning. She would not relinquish scheduling and hiring to someone else, even if others are called on for their insights.

Though filling positions and completing the master schedule can be done quickly, she knows that being efficient in these tasks is not the same thing as being effective. Effective hiring and coaching of teachers will require that she be the lead teacher in her building. It is important to note that principals struggle to hire the best teachers when they are not experts themselves in great teaching. They must be instructionally sound, to the core.

The principal at this school would ensure that each child who did not read well would be mentored, nurtured, challenged, and monitored routinely. She would know each child by name, and not just by number. The principal would ensure that all children and their parents knew the skills the children lacked and they would set ambitious goals together. The school faculty, families, and community agencies would be fully aligned in their support for each student, with activities and outcomes designed to ensure that no child leaves elementary school not ready for middle school.

A principal with an instructional soul would invest in school experiences built around children, culture, and family. The books the children read and the lessons they complete would connect to their passions, cultures, and (yes) families in profound ways. In this manner, the leader would establish systems that empower individuals (ironically enough) and ensure success at all costs. To the students, their school would not feel disconnected from their families and neighborhoods. To the school, the students would feel more like family.

CASE IN POINT: STUDENT ENGAGEMENT/VOICE

Key Dilemma

One of the most pressing challenges facing school leaders today is how to increase student engagement in our classrooms and ensure a greater degree of ownership or agency on the part of each child. We all feel the push to increase the amount of time our students are discussing content and reduce the amount of lecture or "teacher-talk" in our classrooms. Despite our best attempts, we have not yet mastered it, and some schools struggle mightily.

While every school leader can proudly point to an example of engagement done well, we do not find high degrees of student-centered learning and student voice across all classrooms all the time. This begs the question yet again about why our best instructional practices are not systematically applied. One hard reality that we must consider (and admit) is that, in many schools, we are rolling out strategies via school leaders who are uncertain about best practices themselves.

Here again, what sounds great during a book study or school improvement meeting ("We're going to increase student discussion and voice in our classrooms") is rendered unlikely in the hands of school leaders who are not instructionally sound. These are difficult considerations for most principals who pride themselves on knowing great instruction when they see it.

Still, we see time and time again that great strategies like peer collaboration and accountable talk are misapplied or underapplied in the hands of teachers and leaders who are not fully clear on what it all means. With so many best practices in play, the misapplication of a strategy can actually decrease learning. Leaders simply cannot allow this to happen.

Key Actions

Our most effective leaders know the *why* behind every strategy long before implementing it, they know *how* the strategy is connected to the other ones they have rolled out, they know *who* in their buildings are the right ones to train others, and they know *which* classrooms need additional support in getting it right.

Certainly, even our strongest leaders cannot do it alone. In fact, true distributed leadership is a key outcome of leading with an instructional soul. Principals must call on their content specialists and instructional coaches to help. Still, here's the rub: our best leaders do not rely on others to be the instructional experts in the absence of their own command of best practices. This also holds true for district leaders.

A principal with an instructional soul thinks systematically. She would not allow an engagement strategy like accountable talk to be carried out by one teacher in one manner and another teacher in another manner. In our best schools, teaching and learning are rarely inefficient. Every teacher and (ready for this?) every student knows what we are trying to teach them and why we are employing the methods we are employing.

This is not always the case in schools. In our rush to employ the latest techniques as quickly as possible, implementation is shortchanged and fidelity is lost. This is compounded in school districts where teachers rush to implement techniques with help from well-meaning assistant principals and principals who do not fully understand themselves why this solution is being implemented or what sound implementation looks like.

In the case of accountable talk or any discussion protocol, it is common to see principals visit classrooms and admire the level of chatter they see before them. The students are seated in pairs or circles and may be taking turns commenting on the lesson or the learning target as the teacher has instructed them to do. Still, only the most skilled principals are attuned to what the students are talking about, the depth of the conversations they are hearing, the connections those conversations have to the lesson of the day, and the time all this is taking.

Leaders with an instructional soul know the difference between idle chatter and deep learning. In the absence of highly evolved, instructional skills (expertise) and deep instructional convictions (core beliefs), assistant principals and principals can lack the capacity and confidence to do their jobs well. In turn, they may describe what they are seeing as engagement when what they are really hearing is a bunch of noise.

In schools with sound instruction and systems, there is no such confusion. Students can tell you what they are learning, and they can do so in their own words (not in the academic language of the teacher). Teachers in such schools can plan for and evaluate authentic student discussion because they cannot imagine lessons that don't include it. Student connections to the content are paramount. Knowing this, teachers create lessons that impact student lives in purposeful ways by requiring students to voice their own learning, connect it to previous content they have mastered, and relate it to the world around them.

KEY DRIVER 1: REVISION SCHOOL LEADERSHIP

This new orientation for designing schools and systems will require our leaders to retrain and think differently. It will require us to move from solving each day's crises and managing people and processes to something much more poetic than that. It will require a higher degree of intellectual leadership and emotional intelligence that is centered on synthesis and sense-making. These more complex leadership demands will require us to understand deeply why some things are going well and some are not and to pick up on the nuances that stand in the way of real progress.

This is what renowned systems scientist Bela Banathy (1992) calls shifting from "managing things" to "managing complexity." Of course, this shift to a deeper, more complex management style for a new century is not unique to education and is already being applied across many industries. If it helps, think of this new way of leading schools and school systems like the shifts we see in professional sports.

What was required of a head coach or general manager twenty or thirty years ago is no more, a shift from managing players and money like a grand Monopoly game (something even a child can master) to balancing the art and science of micro-statistics, player personas, social media platforms, and the team's entertainment and community engagement brand (something only an accomplished leader can handle).

Systems researcher Blane Despres (2004) likens this leadership approach to the way a veteran teacher might handle a student who is acting out in class. Despite the student's outburst, the master teacher handles the disruption without a hitch, without getting off task, by keeping her eye on the lesson, and by managing this type of daily crisis through a systemic approach.

The master teacher knows that she has no hope of winning the day if she battles each student each day, if she tries to win every encounter, all the while juggling each crisis as it arises. Instead, she knows that all children will stay engaged and learn if she puts systems into place that help her build relationships with her students, anticipate problems before they arise, and quickly remedy small issues without taking her focus (and theirs) off of learning.

To put this another way, our best teachers know that crises arise daily in schools, and as such, the crisis is not the problem at all. Our best teachers realize that if things go awry, they are the problem. Their actions alone impact all outcomes, namely student learning. The teacher is the one who must adapt (not the children), and if she does so successfully, all students will thrive.

Of course, our school systems and the leaders who run them would do well to learn from teachers such as these. If so, they would find that our students and parents are the not the problems and, alas, nor are the teachers within our schools. The system itself is the problem, the one we created. As leaders, we are the ones who must change because our students, parents, and teachers are not going to (nor should they).

Think of it this way: If we could rid ourselves today of every challenge we face in education, every bad policy, every lousy teacher, even every struggling student, we would still be no better off. Why? Because the challenges we face will just come back again. Because the system created the bad policy, the lousy teacher, and even the struggling student. And it will do so again.

LEADERSHIP FOR A NEW GENERATION

If we are to take advice from our best teachers and leaders, from the best research on organizational behavior, and from what our business partners are telling us, then our principals and district leaders (like our students) will require a more complex set of skills for the twenty-first century. This new way of leading will demand greater expertise in teaching and learning, and that it be deeper, wider, and more nuanced. It will demand that our leaders are lifelong learners. Creative. Curious. Inspirational. Transformational.

To pinpoint the skills required of our leaders in a more exacting manner, the following attributes are provided as a way of framing this new psychology of school leadership.

- Facility
- Empathy
- Dexterity
- Ingenuity

Facility/Facilitating Instructional Change

> fa-cil-i-ty (*noun*)—1. *readiness, skill, the means by which something can be done.* 2. *the absence of difficulty.* 3. *aptitude; intelligence; especially across a variety of disciplines.* 4. *credibility.*

Our next-generation leaders must be well grounded in the best of best practices and be experts in our field of teaching and learning. We can no longer afford to hire school principals or district leaders who are not experts in the art, science, and practicality of great teaching. Those days are over. It is not enough that our leaders know "just enough" to discuss teaching with teachers and to fake it through a job interview.

This instructional expertise will be a critical component in building trust with stakeholders (especially teachers) and in leading with authenticity and credibility. At the end of the day, our students and staff must look to school leaders as key advisers and trust that they know what they're talking about. As school and district leaders, we will never be successful in creating great schools if the people we work with don't believe what we are telling them.

In fact, it might be true that the struggles we see among some school leaders (even the struggles they have in building strong relationships) may be tied to their insecurities about instruction, their lack of knowledge around best practices, and their fears about what they do not know.

Empathy/Fostering Meaningful Relationships

> em-pa-thy (*noun*)—1. *ability to share in another's emotions, thoughts.* 2. *identification with other's feelings.* 3. *appreciation of differences that builds understanding, rapport, trust.* 4. *compassion, warmth.*

Our next-generation leaders must genuinely enjoy interacting with students and their families and co-planning alongside their teachers. Empowering teachers, students, and even families to lead will be a key driver to deeper ownership of learning activities. Schools must be built around kids and their families, and so we must make learning more personal and relevant.

This will require leaders to have authentic, organic interactions with students and families and for teachers to design lessons, assignments, projects, and assessments that excite and empower children. Students must see themselves in the work and that will require principals to see themselves in the children.

Schools must be more focused on projects and assessments that tell us what we are good at (asset focused) and that will require principals who see the strengths in their students and teachers long before they see any weaknesses (deficit focused). Such schools must be built around strong teachers, with trust as the centerpiece. This is critical to the success of our work, for school should be something that happens not *to* teachers but *with* teachers, and not *to* children but *for* children.

Dexterity/Navigating Community Connections

> dex-ter-i-ty (*noun*)—1. *keen ability to use one's hands, body, or mind.* 2. *acute mental awareness; adroitness.* 3. *cleverness; agility.* 4. *deft in navigating people, places.* 5. *finesse; artistry.*

The future will require next-generation leaders who can create systems that align and blend all learning activities and outcomes across disciplines and within the lives of our children and families, both in and out of school. This will demand a full integration of departments, subjects, curriculum, and assessments within the school and across our communities and neighborhoods.

In fact, we have to wonder if we can ever expect our students to be social entrepreneurs and renaissance thinkers if they are taught by content experts who rarely collaborate, in school buildings separated by subjects, in local communities separated by walls and fences, and via departments that are siloed.

Leading with an instructional soul will require us to create schools where there are clear connections between life and lessons. These lessons must inspire and inform our students' plans for their lives and give clarity to the things they long to answer. Make no mistake. Like adults, all children seek wisdom, even if they do not know what that is yet. They seek belonging and purpose and self-actualization.

Our students see glimpses of these things in nature, among their families and friends, and across their communities. They just don't find such connections at school. The future will demand that our leaders have the ability to connect the dots across systems and the agility to work with teachers, families, mentors, and mayors to make it all work.

Ingenuity/Seeing around the Bend

> in-ge-nu-i-ty (*noun*)—1. *the quality of being inventive, ingenious.* 2. *especially cunning in solving problems.* 3. *talent, flair for staying current.* 4. *resourcefulness; cleverness, enterprising.* 5. *wisdom.*

Across our next-generation schools, success will come for school leaders who can articulate and carry out the most creative distribution of ideas and resources. Whatever our schools become in the future, the education market will be highly competitive and grossly saturated. Every conceivable concept of schooling will be proposed, whether it falls under a label of public, private, charter, or something else. Technology will push us in exciting ways. Standards and accountability measures will shift. Family engagement and involvement will be paramount.

All of this will require next-generation leaders who can see around the bend. Some bold ideas will be explored via this book, though many, many more will follow in the coming years. We will need leaders who can manage that degree of change, bring about new innovations of their own, and build capacity among teachers and staff to make it happen. This will require leaders who don't settle for the status quo, who strategically enter and exit from current trends, and who stay attuned to the marketplace and relevant to their consumers.

THE MAP IS NOT THE TERRITORY: APPLIED

Let us revisit here the argument made in the previous chapter that we cannot employ our solutions or strategies one student or one teacher at a time, nor rewrite the same improvement plans over and over and expect lasting change. This is why developing schools with a soul only *begins* with a soulful leader but *ends* with a systematic redesign of what we want our schools to be, a system with high expectations for every teacher and child, and with full alignment of our lessons, strategies, and processes.

Along the way, let us be reminded that developing this compelling redesign is not the solution we seek, for the map is just the map. We don't seek a plan to redesign our schools. We want our schools to *be* redesigned. Even more than that, we want this redesign to be so pervasive that it becomes not a *re*design but *our* design. For the map is just the map, not the territory.

Before we explore this any further, it is important that we avoid falling into the trap of "So what?" or "We're already doing that." To help counter this reaction, let us stop for a moment and imagine what is really happening in our schools, in most classrooms on most days, if we were providing an honest assessment. Fair or not, let's provide a mental model of what most classrooms look like on most days in most school districts.

Most teachers in most classrooms are bravely mired in skill-building or test prep or "standards" prep with a healthy dose of classroom management challenges thrown in, topped with lessons provided by or approved by someone else, whiteboard configurations that matter more to visitors than to kids, and a clock in their heads (or sometimes an actual clock) that keeps them moving along at such a frenetic pace that they don't feel empowered to do much otherwise.

For these teachers, the thought of engaging in meaningful, purposeful, and rigorous activities with their children is not likely, and even if it is, it is a function of one teacher's ambition to push further than it is the system's design for deeper learning. We can blame all of this on the state or the district office or the principal or the teacher, but this picture of our classrooms is typical, and the frustrations are real.

Yes, yes, it is true. We have many exceptions. We have many, many master teachers and model classrooms across all school districts. Still, they remain the exception. That's why we call them "models." The prideful notion we hear from some principals and district leaders that many (or most) of their classrooms are centers for engaging dialogue around real-world problems and that we are producing highly skilled writers, orators, engineers, and scientists is simply not typical. Even if we can point to some exemplar classrooms and lessons, we can find just as many that are not rigorous, not engaging, and not innovative.

PIONEER SPECIES: THE CONSEQUENCE OF LEADERSHIP

In making this new reality authentic, we must demand that our leaders clearly define a vision for what we want schools and systems to be. In doing so, we should be clear that there is much at stake in whatever we decide. And let us not fool ourselves. In fact, let us be exceedingly clear that there is much at stake here, both for the present and future of our schools as we know them.

In fairness, we must try to view this idea of a robust new school system as very much possible and avoid the hyperbole that is proffered through many articles and texts and by nearly all politicians and policy-makers. This book will not join many others in offering an end-of-time prophecy, though that is what some critics of our public schools do espouse.

Though it is true that systems must evolve to avoid extinction, this book does not suggest that a day will come where we will no longer have a public school system (though it may be much, much smaller), nor does it suggest that we won't have model schools (though there may be many, many fewer). What is being suggested here is not the end of public schooling, but something much, much worse.

It is an unfortunate reality that our evolution as schools and school systems into fully integrated systems of high expectations, innovation, and social action has been too slow and, at times, nonexistent. If this continues, we will see a day when our schools and school systems will become less relevant (maybe irrelevant), less appreciated (maybe unappreciated), less inspiring (maybe uninspiring), and less necessary (maybe unnecessary).

The only antidote is you.

Leaders have always had the capacity to change the course of history. In keeping with our theme of the *ecology* of change, let's focus a moment on the science of "ecological succession." In short, ecological succession is what we call the change process that an ecological community goes through over time. To picture this, try to imagine the expansive wilderness of the northwest, maybe somewhere in the far reaches of Montana.

A small, isolated community of plants grows over time (through thousands of years) into a complex, self-governing, vibrant ecological community. This community may continue, seemingly unchanged, for generations (like a school system, for instance). Until. Until. Something happens. It can be a small disturbance or a catastrophic event. In our example, this could be a fire or a landslide or a new species. In any case, something happens. In fact, something *always* happens. It is inevitable.

What comes next matters most. The first brave species to emerge after that change event, even after the most catastrophic events, are called "pioneer species." These new species are different somehow, hardy and bold and ready to start anew. They don't wait around. They move in and colonize the damaged ecosystem, the first step in a continuum of ecological succession that leads to an even stronger, more stable, and more diverse ecosystem.

Think of it as the benefit to the system for starting anew, as a return on leadership or the consequence of leadership. In fact, we might define this "consequence of leadership" as one's responsibility to alter his own environment and that of others, to provide a subtle disturbance or catastrophic event that forces a change that will (if strategically conceived) result in a stronger, more stable, and more diverse system.

In this process of ecological succession, new life forms in places that were formally barren. One such stage is called primary succession, the establishment of new habitats where there were none previously (going where no habitat has gone before). The other stage is called secondary succession, the regeneration of life for a community that has been reshaped following one of these change events (a vibrant, new habitat that is stronger than the one before).

This new life formed through ecological succession evolves from a few pioneering species into a climax community of increased diversity and mass that, in turn, provides a greater resistance to invasive species in the future. The system is more mature than it was before, better equipped to take on future changes, and ready to maximize all the resources at its disposal. The system is stronger than ever, confident, nimble, and quicker to react to and recover from the inevitable forces that are out to destroy it.

Let us endeavor to unearth such a system for our schools.

Stronger than ever. Confident and nimble. All we need now are a few pioneering leaders and some rich damn soil.

Chapter Three

The "So What" of Systems Change

The kids would notice first. If we were ever to create schools where lessons and projects and interactions were authentic and aligned, the kids would notice right away. We wouldn't have to ask them. They would notice immediately, like when we change the lines in the lunchroom or switch out the sodas in the vending machines. In fact, the push and pull of innovation in our schools would be so stark that there might be resistance at first, mostly because human nature causes us to resist those things that we do not recognize and cannot fathom.

For both our students and teachers, repurposing our schools for a new generation might feel as if we have switched out the sodas in the vending machines with sirloin steak and Cheez Whiz. A seismic shift in what we call schooling and learning would impact our children the way the internet, social media, and self-driving cars overturned our realities during the past decades. Each innovation was thrust on us seemingly out of nowhere and was unimaginable at the time. We would have the same reaction if we ever dared to reimagine our schools.

In fact, if we could dig deep and unearth right now a profound school experience for our children, what we would discover would be so far removed from what we know now that we wouldn't understand it at first. We might not even appreciate it. That is why writers pivot to metaphors about going to the moon. We all need mental models like that to help us grasp that which is beyond our imaginations. The presiding metaphor in this text for establishing such a system is a *soul*, for every great cause there ever was, and every great victory that was ever won, first had a soul.

Our modern educational system lacks such a thing. This charge is not made to characterize any one school or school system, nor to unfairly minimize the heroic people who serve our children. Across school districts everywhere, many of our teachers and leaders are fully on board with such innovations. Still, even as educators express big ideas and strong beliefs about what is required to engage all children, our professional decisions do not always reflect those beliefs and our systems almost never do. Again, our paradox emerges.

In fact, stop and think about that for a moment. Even those teachers and leaders who are morally attuned to the changes required often lack the position, authority, or resolve to orchestrate such shifts even when they are called for. Why so many are hesitant to change and what we do about it are not easy things to sort through, though this text will root out some possibilities and solutions.

A couple of examples are in order to help us deepen our understanding of what is meant by truly innovative systems. So, we will restate here the point made in previous chapters that all the ecosystems in all the world are interconnected (yes, like a web or wheel), and all of the parts are designed in some ways (even if they are flawed) to serve the whole. The solutions then around dramatic and lasting school improvement must take us back to the whole or, more accurately, to the center of our school systems.

What do we really stand for? What mandates genuinely drive our work? We have to answer questions like these, no matter how long it takes, because these are the narrow portals through which decisions are made. In doing so, we will find out that any system (even if it is flawed) can function each day with little to no interruption, seemingly on autopilot, even without a well-formed center. But only a system with a strong core can function successfully.

Let us look at two simple examples to get us closer to the point.

- *A school has decided to remodel its cafeteria.* The students want more room to eat and visit with their friends. They have even suggested that some extra tables would help, so they can spread out their books and start on their homework. The custodians want tables and chairs that are easy to clean and stack, all designed to make their jobs easier and more efficient. The cheerleading coach wants enough room to practice in the lunchroom after school, and the math coach wants a projector installed so she can lead trainings there from time to time.
- *A school has hired a new family engagement coordinator.* The district has funded the new position and is requiring each school to establish a family engagement team. The superintendent wants these teams to make families feel welcome in schools and keep them involved and informed. The principal wants the new coordinator to handle a variety of tasks that the front office staff and counselors used to do, from signing up more volunteers to putting on the back-to-school program and open-house events. The coordinator and her new team are not sure of their purposes, but they agree that

more parents should be on campus for school events. In not knowing where to turn, the coordinator establishes a parent booster organization and makes that her primary task for the new year.

The two narratives provided above are not unfamiliar to anyone who has worked in schools. In fact, both are playing out today in school districts everywhere. It may appear to most that neither the remodeling of the cafeteria nor the establishment of a family engagement team has much to do with the day-to-day rigors of teaching reading and arithmetic. That is precisely the point.

With layers upon layers of mandates and pressures put on teachers and leaders, it is no wonder why someone wants to get a task like remodeling the cafeteria over with as quickly as possible and not confuse it with the more serious dilemmas facing our schools. This is true, of course, except for the enduring reality that the decisions about which books to read, which technology programs to purchase, and which policies and practices will improve student attendance are often treated with the same "let's just get this over with" response that we hear regarding the cafeteria remodeling.

This response has little to do with any lack of commitment or professionalism on the part of educators. On the contrary, it has much more to do with a lack of understanding and synergy around why any of it matters. Though schools and school districts can point to a person here or there who feels fully responsible for one initiative or another, we rarely tap into the collective will necessary to see dramatic improvement across schools and subjects. Nothing we do feels truly gravitational. Nothing is spiritual.

The most obvious barrier to progress is the very real challenge of balancing too many things. Most school leaders will not admit this publicly, but will relay privately their frustrations caused by managing too many initiatives on any given day. Of course, this is not unique to education. A 2018 article in the *Harvard Business Review* titled "Too Many Projects" warns that leaders across all industries find it increasingly difficult to turn down new ideas and sunset others. "Instead, leaders keep layering on initiatives, which can lead to severe overload at levels below the executive team" (Hollister and Watkins, 2018).

When leaders complain about such things, they are describing not only too many projects, but also a lack of alignment among them or a belief that they overlap with others already in place. Of course, this happens more frequently in organizations where executives and their teams are departmentalized and siloed. "Most senior leaders have a line of sight into their own groups' initiatives and priorities but a limited view of other groups' activities. Because functions and units often set their priorities and launch initiatives in isolation, they may not understand the impact of neighboring functions and units" (Hollister and Watkins, 2018).

If we lean on organizational theory for support, we will find that the actions we put in place in our schools will serve teachers and children best (and impact learning more) if they are intentional and not so random. We see time and time again that dramatic gains are possible in organizations where true alignment exists and where very few actions are viewed as "one more thing" to check off the list. This is not just true for schools. The same can be said about effective school districts, there among the tangle of projects managed by our central office staffs.

In school systems with a soul, every decision can and should be made with student achievement in mind, and with efficiency and intentionality around learning. Whatever decision is made around remodeling the cafeteria or establishing a family engagement team is fine and dandy, as long as the decision is made with one end in mind: student learning. In our best schools and districts, learning is not accidental. It is by design. For let us not forget that learning in schools is never lucky.

CLEANING UP OUR MESS: MANAGING YOUR AVERAGE KETCHUP CRISIS

Lest some people think that schools are solely about reading, writing, and arithmetic, we should set the record straight. The academic outcomes we espouse are only the ones we find in school brochures, on the district's website, or among the superintendent's talking points. The day-to-day realities of school and district management are just as likely to revolve around more pressing issues like rerouting bus schedules, fist fights in the courtyard, monthly fire drills, or running down enough substitute teachers to get through the day.

Of course, this is exaggerated slightly to make a point because it is true that we still find time to teach reading and math (sometimes quite effectively) once we get the other more pressing matters checked off our lists. To complete our descent from the strange to the ridiculous, let us consider a recent example of a school leadership team that was frustrated about the number of ketchup packets the students were using and then leaving on the floor at the end of lunch.

In an administrative meeting called to solve this crisis (yes, there was actually a meeting called), the principal, assistant principals, and cafeteria manager debated for some time how best to keep the pervasive packets in check. Most of the solutions offered were around punishing the kids, including one ingenious suggestion that federal Title 1 monies be used to purchase hidden cameras. Of course, absent from the meeting were (wait for it) the students and (wait for it again) the custodians who swept up the packets each day. No one even thought about inviting them.

With no actionable solution in place, the meeting was adjourned to great consternation. A few days later, when word of the meeting made its way to the head plant operator, a dedicated custodian solved the crisis in just a few seconds. His answer? Don't use ketchup packets. Place two or three large ketchup pump stations around the cafeteria to provide easy access for the kids and a more centralized mess for the team to clean up. A one-minute conversation. Problem solved.

There is so much in play in this one innocuous example that sets the tone for so many things we need to address in our schools, the most important being this: we are not always singularly and collectively focused on student achievement, and the systems are not in place to make that so. It is important that we pause here for a moment because there is no reason to read on if we cannot agree on that point. In fact, there is no greater lesson to be learned from this text.

Though oversimplified to make a point, we must agree that the day-to-day operations and decisions in school districts are hindered by chaos and crisis and are undermined by structures of our own making. As a result, the realities and challenges of the day win out too many times, and achievement suffers.

Let us get back to our examples to render a firsthand look of why this is.

Cafeteria Remodeling—Re-Examined

We will use the remodeling of the cafeteria to make the point that student achievement is not always number one. We will use the cafeteria space precisely because it appears to be far removed from the important matters happening in math and reading classrooms. Here is what we know for sure.

No matter who decides on what the school should do with its cafeteria, it is likely to rest with adults and with little or no involvement from students. It is likely that the wishes of adults to make the cafeteria easier to clean will win out over the wishes of students to create a better study space. Even if we add a few extra tables to satisfy the kids, the adults and their needs most often come first.

Of course, let us be clear here that no one wants to be unsupportive of the dedicated men and women who work to keep our campuses clean. We should certainly gather their opinions as to the best tables to purchase in support of a clean and efficient lunchroom.

In the same way that we want to resolve our ketchup-mess decisions with the custodians in the room, we want to make facility and curriculum decisions with teachers and students in mind. In fact, it is hidden deep within countless day-to-day decisions such as these that a sad reality emerges: Our schools do not always operate efficiently in impacting instructional outcomes as much as we do operational ones.

If we could slow down long enough to consider it, we would admit that we often view things like facilities planning, teacher hiring, athletic events, and even master scheduling, as loosely aligned practices and not as strategic initiatives designed to impact learning in *direct* ways. In fact, we might find that the assistant principal in charge of facilities or athletics and the head plant operator at any given school are unaware of the reading and math goals and initiatives and do not feel connected to the larger mission of student achievement.

We have to wonder what great ideas would emerge if only we involved them and others like them. Someone might suggest that the school install study carrels in the cafeteria to provide additional homework space or more computer stations for students to do research or check their grades. Heck, the cafeteria remodeling project might not even resemble a cafeteria when completed, as much as it might resemble a coffee house or creative instructional space.

So why use such a remote example as remodeling the cafeteria? Only to make this point: Though we would all admit that getting our custodians and bus drivers connected to the larger mission of student achievement is a nice concept, we would be troubled to find that there are many other employees in our schools and district offices who operate in equally discordant ways as they race from one decision to the next. And here's the thing. These employees have titles like *teacher*, *instructional coach*, *principal*, and *superintendent*.

Family Engagement Team — Re-Examined

The family engagement team, per our example, has just gotten underway, and the members are already getting mixed signals as to their purpose. Some leaders are demanding better customer service while others want improved PTA attendance. This is not uncommon. Though the members of the new team want to do a great job, and everybody favors getting more parents involved, the fledging group has been given no clear direction. So they are simply diving in.

Even a meeting with the principal or the PTA president may not help, with each of these leaders operating through their own lens of success. In fact, the PTA president is most interested in having the family engagement team help with the school's primary fundraiser in an attempt to finally, finally win the district's coveted PTA program award. The principal is happy with that idea or with anything that makes her school look good and keeps the new family engagement team busy, satisfied, and out of her office.

Of all the ideas tossed around, no one connects the parent engagement efforts to student achievement. No one seriously considers pouring over the sixth-grade math scores on the district formative assessments and setting up a math club or tutoring group directly aimed at those middle-of-the-road math students who (with some added incentive and acceleration) could advance and jump into Algebra 1 by eighth grade.

No one thinks about the family engagement team's role in teaching the parents of those middle-of-the-road math students about a free math website that tracks their child's readiness for Algebra 1. And so it goes. Another decision made. Another opportunity lost. This school and its new parent engagement team are not at fault, for they are like many others. Either the system has let them down or, more likely, there was no system in place to begin with.

STRATEGIC PLANNING: ADDING BY SUBTRACTING

The examples provided above do not represent the most damning struggles facing our school systems. They are simply provided to underscore some of the many taxing initiatives that are costing time and money, not because they are unimportant but because they are disconnected. Strangely, this is made more challenging because of educators themselves. As public servants who are in a rush to fix all things, educators are quick to take on too many solutions in a chaotic attempt to leave no idea unspoken and no innovation untried.

The constant drum of continuous improvement, along with oppressive accountability measures, have compelled us to try everything, to write it all down into a plan, to invent measures we never had before, and to assign department heads to monitor our maze of solutions. From high above, the maze appears connected, even symmetrical. While inside the maze, it is hard to see what is around the next corner, and it is easy to get lost, turned around, and convinced that there is no way out.

The answer to this dilemma is one that is hard for school and district leaders to say out loud. We need to do less and do it well. We need to find a way to do less better. Someone has got to say it: "No. Enough is enough. We are not going to do that. We already have enough initiatives that we believe in. Let's focus on getting those right first." We can be much more efficient by creating connections among our initiatives and/or by not doing some at all.

- "I'm sorry, but our school is going to get our reading scores right. We are going to do reading well. All of our students are going to read and write at very high levels. I promise you that. So, no, we're not going to add that elective right now."
- "Yes, yes. We'd love to, but we are not going to take part in the PTA's healthy schools campaign this year. It sounds great, but don't sign us up

for that grant. We could use the money, but we fear that the grant requirements will take too much time away from our reading initiative."

Though most school and district leaders are strong supporters of strategic planning and project management, we rarely see either done successfully. In support of a systems approach, it seems that the process and products around strategic planning might be enhanced by including both "actions" and "inactions" to narrow the scope of our work to only a few things that we must get right.

Though strategic plans always include "actions"—things we're going to do—it is prudent to also include "inactions"—things that we're going to avoid or things that are outside our capacity as a team. To help us along, let's introduce two terms that are intended to capture the critical aspects of building strategic momentum and, at times, slowing it down.

- *strategic commotion* (actions): specific, intentional, and measurable actions or deliverables that generate high-fidelity collaboration to directly impact organizational culture and outcomes.
- *strategic restraint* (inactions): specific, intentional, and measurable actions or deliverables that are not executed (or delayed) because they distract from or could limit the growth of organizational culture or outcomes.

Let's say that a school district is serious about implementing a targeted, intentional action plan to help African American boys improve their reading or math abilities. If so, the district could certainly place a great deal of time and energy into these efforts over the coming year(s), and with much dedication and high intentionality, scores would surely improve.

So here's the rub.

The district might have to put off for now the idea that a school board member just proposed about helping more students gain access to careers in engineering by investing in districtwide STEM clubs. Yes, some may consider it heresy (and possibly career suicide) to dismiss the school board member, though this example is not meant to pit one good idea against another.

This is just another way of saying that strategic choices have to be made. In making such decisions, it should be clear that there are many ways of showing strategic restraint without going all in on some things and saying no to all other things (especially when it comes to a school board member).

In this example, a strategic decision might be to continue the district's heavy emphasis on the reading initiative, as there is great pressure to improve reading scores, especially among minority children, and still support the school board member by beginning a small, pilot program to gauge the interest and effectiveness of such clubs. There may also be options to align the two ideas or to rally the school board member to the reading cause and (for now) away from the STEM initiative.

Even our best leaders will admit that this is a tough skill to master. Some will argue that we cannot say no, that there is too much pressure upon us to say no to politicians, parents, and business partners. Of course, this is entirely the purpose of showing strategic restraint, even to the point of saying, "Yes, it's a great idea. But, no, we are not taking it on right now. We hope you understand." Some leaders would call this line of thinking unrealistic or naïve. Others might give it another name: *leadership*. For leadership demands hard choices, even unpopular ones.

This is all made easier when we operate from a set of core beliefs from which consistent and purposeful decisions are made. In their book on high-performing school systems, Curtis and City (2015) provide great counsel and fair warning to leaders who jump on every proposal. "The result, paradoxically, is a strategic plan without a strategy. District staff work hard rather than smart, exhausting themselves with pockets of success and lots of wasted effort. Ultimately, students suffer" (p. 3).

As for those who consider this line of thinking naïve, that is certainly fair. As long as we can agree that it is equally naïve to think we are fixing things by taking on too many ideas, by jumping on every bandwagon, by doing many of them poorly, and by convincing ourselves that no one is noticing.

ORGANIZATIONAL ECOLOGY: ADDRESSING THE ENTHUSIASM GAP

Finding the proper balance for when to stir things up (commotion) and when to slow things down (restraint) is the just-right mixture for successful endeavors. School district leaders would do well to learn from those who have orchestrated successful ventures and the hard lessons gleaned from those who were once on top and didn't evolve fast enough to stay there.

This is a good time to remind us that our school districts are large and influential companies in their own rights. Many school districts are among the largest employers in their communities. As such, districts have a unique opportunity to lead others in designing new business models that emphasize and energize people (the business we are in) toward a common cause. In fact, if school districts are serious about being centerpieces for innovation and learning, they must be front and center in leading organizational trends and not just following them.

It is with this in mind that we review our current school and district structures as a means for creating opportunities for stakeholders to interact, for narrowing our focus, and for inspiring a genuine camaraderie in pursuit of strategic outcomes. This can be a particularly messy discussion point for leaders as they evaluate the current state of affairs in their districts and formulate next steps for lasting improvement.

Some critical reflection will be required. Why do many of our employees, students, and parents feel disconnected from each other and from our strategic outcomes? Would a system designed to build stronger human connections, dialogue, and debate lead to healthier climates? Would any of this impact achievement outcomes?

Across most school districts, it is not surprising to find that neither our employees nor our students are as interested or invested in district achievement outcomes as our leaders. Let's consider a couple of scenarios in making this point. When student achievement scores are released, who in your school district races to see them first? When the annual climate survey results come in, who pores over them in search of what is right or wrong in our schools? District leaders? Curriculum specialists? Teachers? Students? Our answers to these questions tell us something about who is really invested in district outcomes and who is tuned out.

In searching out new solutions, this enthusiasm gap must be addressed. Research findings across many industries reach similar conclusions: There is rarely a successful business model that positively impacts outcomes that doesn't positively impact employee relations and well-being in addition. With that said, constructing systems with a soul will require that we reenergize our employees, involve them in problem-solving, and inspire them to lead. Yes, authentic teacher leadership must also be at the heart of this reform.

The emerging research from our partners in organizational behavior science provides school districts with some intriguing insights. The lessons gleaned from Positive Organizational Scholarship (POS) are especially notable in making the case for deeper, richer workplace experiences as a way of impacting measurable outcomes. Think of this new psychology as the science of positivity. Studies regarding the ecology of human relationships within the workforce point to the following four qualities of successful employees: self-efficacy, hope, optimism, and resiliency.

Though this may be difficult to consider, it is fair to wonder whether our current school and district hierarchies are designed to tamp down such things as employee and student self-efficacy and resiliency or relegate them to second-tier status. If this is even somewhat true, it will require some honest soul-searching on the part of leaders about who is creating the systems we have now and who is benefitting from them. No matter who or what is to blame for our shortcomings in climate and culture, there appears to be only two broad conclusions that we can reach:

1. We have not created sufficient structures that foster collaboration, energy, and enthusiasm among stakeholders related to system outcomes.
2. We have not created system outcomes that cultivate collaboration, energy, and enthusiasm among stakeholders.

SYSTEMS APPROACHES: A FAMILIAR MIRAGE

Make no mistake. Our deepest struggles in schools are solvable. We can absolutely teach every child to read. We can absolutely graduate every child. If we set up functioning systems with those outcomes in mind, our schools could absolutely make good on those promises. We have the talent to do so, even if we sometimes lack the will. The problem is, those who work within the system are oftentimes too entrenched to see the possibilities before them.

In his enticing article "How Systems Thinking Applies to Education," Frank Betts (1992) provides a cogent argument on why that is. Perception is the primary problem. He claims that most school leaders will tell you they are managing things efficiently and systematically, while most are not. Most believe they are doing the right things among so many right things, while nodding affirmatively when anyone asks if their plans are aligned and effective. Alas, our leaders cannot see the system for the trees.

As one might expect, the result is more of the same: a system stuck in the muck. Even when leaders boldly espouse change and reform, they get frustrated quickly, abandon their bold ideas, and return to the comforts of conventional schooling. Betts (1992) calls this "pattern maintenance," clinging to age-old routines that we find in schools related to teaching core subjects and providing custodial care to children. Though there is nothing offensive about these things, we have to question whether we are getting any better at doing them and whether our "status quo" curriculum and "status quo" caregiving are enough to meet the new demands of a new society.

In the marketplace of schooling, we have to wonder how long it will take for some other agency to come along and teach our children better than we can and provide topflight day care as well. An aggressive takeover by a more innovative company has happened in every other industry, and it just might happen in our own. The eroding of school systems was prophesied more than twenty years ago by Bela Banathy (1991), a giant in the world of systems alignment and educational change.

In his hallmark text, *Systems Design of Education: A Journey to Create the Future*, he recounts the stories of systems that are not changing with the times and warns of pending entropy, beginning with what he calls "paradigm paralysis." Banathy (1991) provides key reasons why our efforts to make a transition to true systems have found little success:

- The piecemeal and incremental approach
- Failure to integrate solution ideas
- Staying within the boundaries of the existing system (not thinking out of the box)

Banathy's characterizations are eerily familiar even today, and yet we continue to subscribe to them. One must start to question whether we continue to attach ourselves to such practices because they work so well or because we have a monopoly on running schools. In fact, substantive research findings tell us that the inefficiencies described by Banathy do not wash with best practice and do not align with continuous improvement models nor backwards design. In fact, many of these tired solutions are sort of like backwards planning but without the design part.

We know that a quality evaluation of any agency, division, or initiative begins with an honest assessment of where it places its priorities. In essence, where does the system expend its energy? We know that any company that values its employees by tending to their needs, asking for their input, and building strong personal connections will likely have a great work culture.

Similarly, any school district that focuses on meeting state mandates (or even financial ones) will likely succeed at those things at the expense of other things. Betts (1992) contends that most school districts focus almost exclusively on legal or political mandates (such as state accountability metrics) and not on social mandates that are just as pressing (such as climate, culture, engagement, and belonging).

REMAINING ALERT: AVOIDING THE TRAPS

Systems falter when leaders succumb to missteps and distractions known as "system traps" (Meadows, 2008). One such trap is losing focus on outcomes in times of chaos or perceived crises. Another occurs when leaders look inward too much, focusing on *their* departmental successes or *their* daily tasks and losing sight of the larger goals the organization. Meadows calls these traps "fixes that fail."

As an example, she recalls the desperate struggle for illegal drug supplies on our city streets. Drug addicts want to have access to large supplies, law enforcement wants to keep it as low as possible, and drug dealers want to keep it right in the middle so prices don't get too high or too low. "The average citizen really just wants to be safe. . . . All the actors work hard to achieve their different goals" (Meadows, 2008, p. 113).

As a result, the interested parties have competing aims, nobody is on the same page, and nothing changes. The solution, of course, combines some part commotion and some part restraint. We must rally people to share in a common cause while avoiding the tendency to take on too much. Interestingly, we don't have to search too far for examples. It is familiar to see this kind of common energy and focus in times of war or tragedy, where communities come together and where hierarchies give way to a greater mission that has no patience for bureaucracy and no time for titles.

This brings us back to the successful principal mentioned in the previous chapter, who was strong enough to stay true to her instructional vision and tune out the rhetoric. She brought two qualities to the table that apply here: (1) a core belief about quality instruction, and (2) a steadfastness to the cause. Most quality principals and district leaders have the first attribute. Only the best possess the second one. With very real social and political pressures facing schools today, it is not hard to understand why this is.

In case some cannot fathom what the holdup is, let's consider what school and district leaders must deal with on a daily basis: impatient bosses, angry parents, media pressures, know-it-all community members, bureaucratic policies, political pressures, natural disasters, man-made disasters, self-imposed crises, budget headaches, state mandates, family pressures. Through all of this, the principal mentioned above remained true to her beliefs and didn't take on extra things that might have pushed her school off course. This a critical leadership quality that is referred to as "filtering the noise" (Curtis and City, 2015, p. 20).

SCHOOL DISTRICT RENOVATION: LEAD, ALIGN, REPEAT

The innovative schools we so desperately seek for our children are difficult to imagine in school districts that operate under the weight of outdated bureaucracies and hierarchies. This is why our current school systems represent both the problems we face and the solutions we seek. This reality should provide district leaders with equal parts trepidation and motivation in taking on the great challenges facing schools today. As previously expressed, this book is not designed as an indictment of the people who serve the system, as we are all victims of the dissonance that we feel. Still, make no mistake. We are also the perpetrators of our own dysfunction.

No matter the school districts we work for, the frustrations we experience are quite the same. They begin like this: somebody wants to reduce disciplinary referrals, so we rally together and focus our collective energies on that. Somebody else is hell-bent on fixing our lousy reading scores, so we rally around that too, putting into place this quick-fix initiative or that one in hopes that something might stick (system trap).

A few days later a student is injured crossing a busy road so safety meetings are held and we adjust the bus stops. The reading program we adopted has just gotten underway, but reviewing our safety plans becomes today's top priority (system trap). While all of that swirls around us, somebody gets tired of our old data system or payroll system or teacher evaluation system, so we stop doing that one and begin vetting another one, all of this with little or no discussion on how these solutions impact other solutions, or current district policies and practices, or student learning outcomes (system trap).

As district leaders chase down every potential solution, school staff are left confused, frustrated, and blurry-eyed in trying to keep it all straight. As a result, some of our best educators and school leaders do not see the connections between their actions and student learning outcomes, not unlike the boy in the back row.

Though every school district knows that teaching and learning is its primary mission, it is also true that there are those working in our schools and district offices right now who would describe their jobs as focused on something else (discipline, attendance, or family engagement to name a few). This does not even count the dozens upon dozens of colleagues who manage advanced data systems or budgeting processes or hiring. Many of those employees do not see the impact of their work on student learning.

There is certainly nothing wrong with any of these job functions, except when you ask these employees about the district's instructional outcomes, and they stare blankly back at you or suggest that there is someone more qualified than they to have that discussion. In school systems with a soul, no employee or department is so confused. Our mission for learning is narrow. Our focus clear.

Why is this focus on learning so important? Because, at the end of the day, no school district wants families to be involved in their schools simply for the sake of family involvement. What all schools want is for all children to learn, and they know that involving families is one way to get there. For the same reason, we don't want fewer suspensions just so we can report having fewer suspensions (though that's always nice). What we all want is for students to learn, and reducing suspensions is one way to get us there. Things like improved student attendance and parent involvement are not goals. They are actions. For learning is the only goal.

TRADITIONS MASKED AS SYSTEMS

Most schools and school districts are built the same way, as vertical hierarchies that are hard to reorient after many years of tradition and so many fixed mindsets. There is certainly nothing wrong with organizational structure (or charts), just as there is nothing magical about one hierarchy (vertical) versus another (horizontal). Still, it is fair to wonder if the mindsets of district and school employees (and their workflows) are impacted by how they perceive themselves within the organization itself. It is also fair to consider whether student learning outcomes are affected by such mindsets.

A quick glimpse at any organizational chart gives each employee a sense of order and place, along with an idea of what is and is not their concern. Organizational charts (as functions of bureaucracy) are designed to provide structure, while also creating boundaries, installing limitations, and isolating ideas. In most cases across most industries, it is common to find that those who work within top-down systems are fixed (or fixated) solely on their assigned roles and job descriptions by providing reports or services to those above and below them, with little understanding of how their actions impact larger system outcomes.

As we contemplate this crisis of perspective, let us picture a leader in any school district who believes in the district's mission and is convinced that he or she is part of an aligned system for improvement. Then, let us consider whether he or she is imagining the system as it *really is* or as it *should be*. Could it be possible that the leader is conjuring up visions of departments working cohesively in pursuit of common district outcomes without any real sense that this is actually occurring? Might we wonder if the images playing out in the leader's head of collaboration among colleagues are simply pictures of a lot of the same people who end up in a lot of the same meetings?

Let's put it this way: Leaders who say that they believe in systems that are aligned and innovative may skew their perspectives in such a way as to believe that their systems are actually doing quite well. Senge (1990) puts it this way: "If non-systemic thinking predominates, the first condition for nurturing vision is not met: a genuine belief that we can make our vision real in the future. We may say, 'We can achieve our vision' (most American managers are conditioned to this belief), but our tacit view of current reality as a set of conditions created by somebody else betrays us" (p. 12).

The complexities of these riddles may be lost on some, mostly because we are too close to the work to see them. Still, our industry is replete with ironies so entrenched that we have to unpack them as part of any problem-solving process. Two such ironies that require our attention are as follows:

1. An industry designed around people (teachers and students) and purely human outputs (skills, intelligence, kindness) has created accountability systems and metrics that seem more suited to building cars than kids.
2. An industry designed to facilitate intellectualism and creativity has created curricula, assessments, and structures designed to limit experimentation, cultural awareness, social interaction, and voice.

KEY DRIVER 2: RESTRUCTURE SCHOOL SYSTEMS

Our current school and district structures are inhibiting our academic progress. We cannot ignore this reality any longer. As we consider possible solutions, we must stay rooted in systems theory and organizational theory in helping us imagine a better way. Still, a word of caution is in order. As we revision such structures, we must be careful to avoid viewing any type of realignment as a quick fix or a literal solution to our problems.

Just as the plan is not the solution, an organizational chart is not either. Any realignment of our workplace should be viewed only as a starting point, as a sparkplug for kick-starting fresh conversations that can lead to more soulful experiences for leaders, teachers, and students around learning outcomes.

We will explore district-level structures in making a case for change, though school hierarchies must follow suit. We will consider the figures below as a way of providing the reader context for how structures contribute to both progress and paralysis. The traditional organizational structure found in most school districts is presented in figure 3.1 as a vertical hierarchy with the superintendent of schools at the top and any number of assistant superintendents and directors below overseeing key departments. This figure is modeled after an organizational chart from a midsized school district in California, though truncated for simplicity.

By contrast, the ones that follow (figures 3.2 and 3.3) show the same basic departments and divisions aligned horizontally in ways that may be more accommodating to system alignment and collaboration. Of course, neither of these alternative options is presented as absolutes. Dozens of organizational shapes are possible if we wish to go there. The ones provided are only meant to challenge our thinking about how structures and work-products might be more cross-departmental in driving student achievement.

The familiar structure shown as figure 3.1 is top-down and highly departmentalized, which can sometimes breed employee isolation and frustration if left unchecked. Though pockets of success can result within more traditional structures, there are also many examples of departments competing for success and attention, led by division heads who are accountable for narrow outcomes that they alone are charged with impacting.

As one example, it is common to find the head of the Human Resources division orchestrating a plan to hire enough qualified teachers to keep both the schools well-staffed and the superintendent happy. The division head is not typically involved in matters of curriculum and instruction in the same way that the district's curriculum leaders are not deeply involved in the hiring of teachers. The same thing goes for the heads of professional development or assessment or technology.

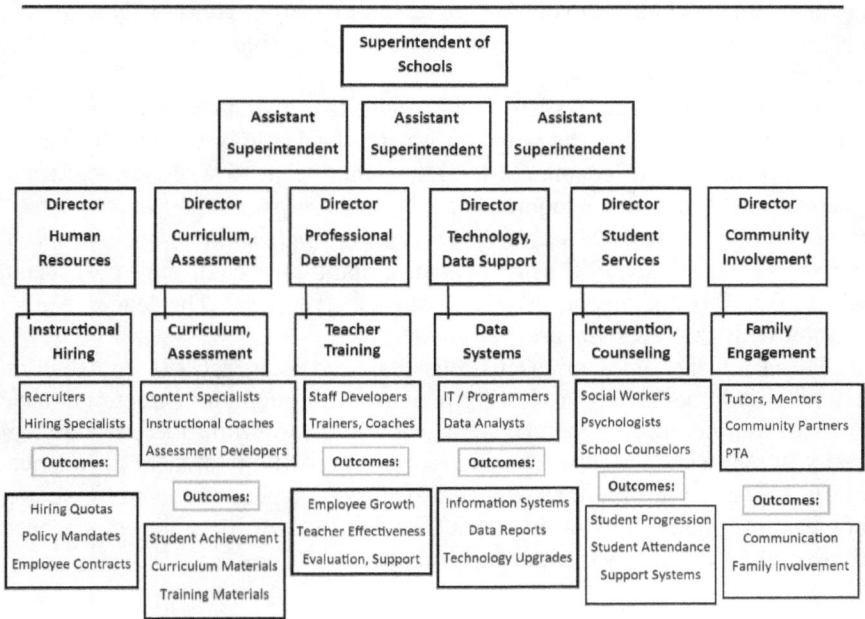

Figure 3.1. District Organizational Chart Example/Vertical
Note: Figure is not presented as a complete organizational chart but as representative of most key departments found within a typical school district. This traditional, vertical chart is modeled after a mid-sized school district in California.

Whoever oversees buses is concerned about buses. Whoever oversees family involvement is concerned about increasing involvement. Each of these important initiatives are critical to school success, though loosely aligned at best. In the end, the day-to-day work can become so focused on keeping the district running that we are less attuned to outcomes that we could collectively impact.

Let's dig deeper to see how these isolated efforts might be connected in more impactful ways. Both attendance and family involvement are familiar examples. We all know that improved student attendance is positively correlated to student achievement. Still, we have to wonder if better attendance is really the endgame. Is it not more accurate to say that student achievement is the endgame and that attendance is just one of many, many drivers in getting us there? If so, might we consider a systems approach to connect student attendance to related performance drivers like family engagement?

In fact, might we posit that student attendance *is* family engagement? We can certainly argue that the two cannot be separated, since getting a child to school is the most important action that a parent can take in supporting education. Is it fair to ask whether the goals of the attendance and family engagement specialists in your school or school district are directly aligned? Could we go further even in requiring that their outcomes be aligned to student achievement metrics?

A systems approach to district challenges like attendance and parent involvement help to align the work to broader academic outcomes. In fact, a systems leader might encourage the attendance team to write an academic goal as its department outcome: *We seek to improve student math performance on the state assessment by increasing student attendance in math classes across all schools.* The attendance committee chair may push back with: "But I'm not responsible for math achievement." The leader would counter with: "Oh, yes you are. We all are."

These are the types of discussions that leaders in schools and district offices should be having in viewing their work through an instructional lens and not an operational one. To be absolutely clear, while there is nothing really wrong with a committee and even goals specific to student attendance or discipline or tutoring or any other critical issue facing our schools, we are not going to make the kind of impact we want to see if we do not connect these initiatives directly to student learning.

SIDEWAY SOLUTIONS: THINKING HORIZONTALLY

Of course, each school and school district are different and each situation requires its own creative solutions. The questions posed here are designed to push leaders to consider how they deploy staff in ways that best support student learning. The horizontal structure presented as figure 3.2 is one such manner.

It is designed to present the benefits of narrowing the system's focus to fewer strategic outcomes and creating work structures that are more collaborative and cross-functional. Like the others in this chapter, this chart is provided in truncated form and is not intended to show the full scope of district operations (though it could be easily adapted to do so). Let's take a closer look.

In keeping with the district's primary mission of providing top-notch instruction, a broader team of professionals is shown under the heading "Instructional Quality." This team would draw on the energies of several departments in hiring and retaining great teachers, providing them with quality curriculum materials, and improving their practice through engaging professional interaction.

No matter how this is structured, the key thing to note in this organizational chart is the blurring of the lines between "Human Resources," "Professional Development," and "Teaching and Learning." This structure offers

The "So What" of Systems Change   63

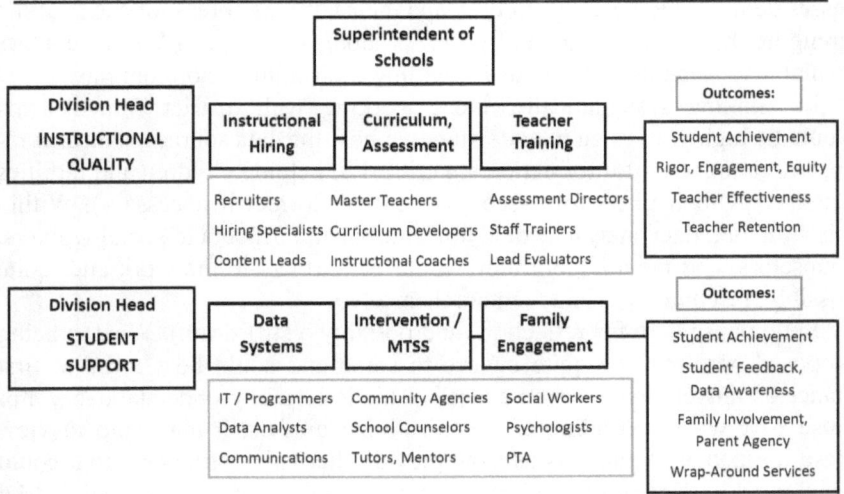

Figure 3.2.   District Organizational Chart Example/Horizontal
Note: **Figure is not presented as a complete organizational chart but as representative of some of the key departments found within a typical school district. It is provided as an adaptation of a traditional, vertical organizational hierarchy.**

subtle differences in comparison to the traditional, vertical hierarchy in the way it aligns outcomes specific to student achievement and teacher effectiveness.

In this school district, employee success is not judged on the quality of the district's curriculum resources or the efficiency of its hiring procedures (though those are important in their own right). Everyone is held accountable for school climate and learning outcomes only. Though the actors listed in each of these charts will differ from district to district, the job titles are meant to represent a singular coalition of employees dedicated to the district's goals of ensuring the highest instructional standards.

As shown in this example, the district's reading, math, science, and social studies experts are just as involved in the hiring and training of teachers as they are in designing and improving district curricula. This approach also calls for stronger teacher leadership in using master teachers as recruiting and hiring specialists and as trainers and mentors. This relationship between master teachers and rookies begins the moment a new teacher signs a contract and lasts until he or she becomes a successful teacher-leader and mentor in his or her own right.

In a similar way, the second row shown in figure 3.2 provides for a larger, collaborative intervention structure for students under the heading of "Student Support." This would codify a powerful alignment of people and processes dedicated to keeping children and their families abreast of each child's strengths, his or her goals and progress along the way, and key supports available to students and parents in tackling each child's shortcomings.

In thinking systematically, those working with district data systems would be highly invested in understanding how the data sources, data accuracy, and timeliness of information are critical in helping children and families better chart their plans for success (or course correct if necessary). Within this structure, data analysts would not simply hand off data to social workers, counselors, and mentors, but they would be partners in the work and, quite possibly, be counselors and mentors themselves.

Let's pause here for reflection (and possibly a stiff drink). What is being proposed here may be quite bizarre to some and could be viewed at first glance as unworkable or even chaotic. This is certainly understandable. For those who work in traditional organizational models, it may help to view these horizontal alignments as examples of alternative structures that could be adopted in parts or pieces if the idea of upending the entire school district is a bit head-scratching.

SIDEWAYS TURNED UPSIDE-DOWN: HORIZONTAL DECISION-MAKING

The organizational structure provided as figure 3.3 is nearly identical to the horizontal chart found above in figure 3.2, with one critical exception. In this chart, the district is led, quite literally, by those who work in our schools and communities. Yes, the school board and superintendent of schools retain final authority, but district decisions are heavily influenced by those on the front lines of learning.

What we call these teams of teachers and principals is inconsequential (committees, professional networks, communities of practice). Whomever serves on them or how they are structured can also be debated and shifted. What matters is that districts with a soul design structures that give principals, teachers, students, and community members substantive voice in the future of our schools. In fact, a true system with a soul would require the lines between job titles to be erased and much larger circles of influence to be penciled in.

While some will struggle with this idea initially, leaders across all industries are coming to grips with a new reality that some are not yet aware of. Employees are already leading without our involvement or even in spite of it. Many of the creative solutions in schools and school districts (even ideas that fail) are being conceived and commissioned by employees far down on the organizational ladder.

This is commonly referred to as "leading up." New ideas are brought forward in a manner that is comfortable for the system. Think of it as the ingenious method that wives use in getting their husbands to clean the leaves out of the gutters or plan a romantic getaway. Unbeknownst to the husband, the savvy wife has been thinking about and planning such things for many, many weeks, dropping hints and stroking his ego, until (alas) he comes along and proclaims one of these ideas as his own.

Schools and school districts would do well to embrace and formalize structures that empower key agents like teachers and students to offer up creative solutions and profound insights to move learning forward. The research around informal and formal "communities of practice" provides a great deal of guidance on how and where to begin. "In particular, it allows us to see past more obvious formal structures such as organizations, classrooms, or nations, and perceive the structures defined by engagement in practice and the informal learning that comes with it" (Wenger and Wenger-Trayner, 2015, p. 3).

Leaders have a clear choice. They can either tap into the energy of employees or pretend it doesn't exist. Oh, and since we remain on irony alert, it should be noted that our best employees (and our worst ones) are already working in teams and networks to champion district causes or to undermine them. They meet in coffee shops, teacher lounges, and online. They are already leading up. Their bosses are just too busy or distracted to notice.

As with all second-order change initiatives, human nature requires that persons find value in the changes being proposed. Leaders are most successful when they assign meaning to change by partnering with those stakeholders most impacted by it and by avoiding the tendency to issue change orders via edicts or emails. "To change the conventional style of management accordingly requires a shift in perception that is anything but easy, but it also brings great rewards. Working with the processes inherent in living systems means that we do not need to spend a lot of energy to move an organization. There is no need to push, pull, or bully it to make it change. Force, or energy, is not the issue; the issue is meaning" (Capra and Luisi, 2014, p. 318).

THE END GAME: STRUCTURES BEFORE STRATEGIES

If we are to ever reinvent our current structures, we should be attentive to changing mindsets long before we tackle things like organizational charts. As we know, creative solutions will fail if not executed in a strategic manner. With this in mind, principals and district leaders can begin right now revisioning the way they *think* about alignment, collaboration, and shared decision-making before they start trying to *improve* them.

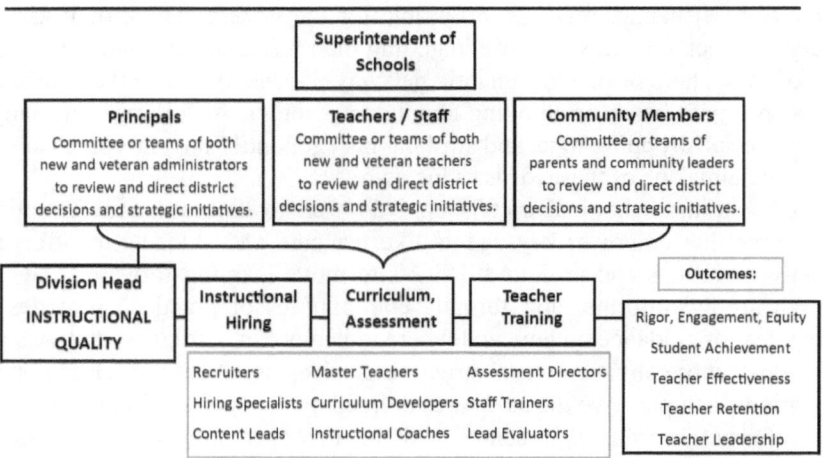

Figure 3.3. District Organizational Chart Example/Horizontal
Note: Figure is not presented as a complete organizational chart but as representative of some of the key departments found within a typical school district. It is provided as an adaptation of a traditional, vertical organizational hierarchy. The departments presented are connected to improved instructional practice.

Leaders must also consider if the employees they serve are ready for such changes. This is another way of saying that we must avoid tossing solutions around without the proper structures and supports in place to make them successful. We have all seen mistakes made when we commission teams and tasks quickly without ensuring full alignment to other initiatives in place. We have also learned from long-standing research and best practice that serious systems failures can arise when an initiative or strategy itself becomes the end, not the means.

In many school districts, it is not uncommon to see entire departments created around a single strategy or grant concept, only to find out later that the fine people who work in the department are so enamored with their work that they are hell-bent on rolling out their project at all costs, even if that means preserving the project itself in spite of more efficient solutions that have come along.

Of course, it doesn't take long before everyone in the district office forgets that the strategy and team were created to improve learning for children, not to create jobs for adults. This is cautionary tale, a screaming example of a system without a soul. Too often, we forget to do what Stephen Covey (2004) reminds us in "keeping the main thing the main thing" (p. 160).

In truth, we don't do this so well. In fact, we find the opposite in many school districts, where an endless array of initiatives and outcomes are measured and tracked as if they are all important (and critical even). Senge (1990) puts it this way: "Since we are part of that lacework ourselves, it's doubly hard to see the whole pattern of change. Instead, we tend to focus on snapshots of isolated parts of the system, and wonder why our deepest problems never seem to get solved" (p. 7).

Leading schools and districts in pursuit of dramatic academic outcomes will require focus and time. There will be no quick fixes. Further, we must know that speaking the words of innovation and change will never be enough. In fact, it never has been. Yes, leadership demands that we actualize our vision. "Vision without systems thinking ends up painting lovely pictures of the future with no deep understanding of the forces that must be mastered to move from here to there. This is one of the reasons why many firms that have jumped on the 'vision bandwagon' in recent years have found that lofty vision alone fails to turn around a firm's fortunes" (Senge, 1990, p. 12).

Whatever solutions we pursue, and however we pursue them, it is prudent for us to be bold in our pursuit. Experience tells us that structures will not be easy to alter, and that mindsets will not be so easy to shift. Research tells us that no lasting change will come without thoughtful planning and implementation. Logic dictates that success will arrive through some combination of smarts, savvy, efficiency, and patience. And our gut tells us what it has told us all along: that the right path to take has always been clear, if only we have the will to choose it.

Chapter Four

A Path to Self-Actualization

No matter what schools look like in the future, success will come when all decisions are made with each student's best interests in mind and with relationships at the core. This will include deep consideration of each child's strengths and passions and even how curricula and lessons are designed to enrich the home lives of children and families. Deeper human connections will be paramount because schools must be focused on developing students socioemotionally and not just academically.

If we do this well, the entire experience of schooling will feel more organic and personal to the boy in the back row, from the relationships he forms with his teachers to the assignments he interacts with. What he learns and how he learns it will make sense to him, and matter to him and his family. Creating such schools will require districts to build systems and processes from the student outward. From the curriculum outward. From the lessons outward. From the core.

All of this will demand bold leadership. It will require districts to recalculate the methods and measures used to track student progress in socio-developmental terms and not only in statistical language like grade point averages and percentile ranks.

It will require schools to measure student success in ways that make sense to children and families and not through the cracked lens of microdata provided by state and district officials (stanines and scale scores by school, by grade level, by teacher, and by subgroup upon subgroup upon subgroup). In schools with a soul, students are viewed as distinctive and expressive human beings, not as percentile ranks.

THE POSSIBILITIES OF SCHOOLING: SCHOOL IN A FUTURE TENSE

In connecting the dots for us, it would be disingenuous to suggest a new way of creating and leading schools and school districts if the system itself was designed to graduate young adults who are essentially soulless, with only minimal skills, no continuity of learning, no sense of themselves, no understanding of the world around them, and no self-mandate to make things better. The reality of our current school model doesn't always mesh with such lofty ambitions. And so the hard work begins for each of us by admitting that our schools are not there yet and that they could be so much more if we tapped into our collective energy and expertise.

Here's the challenge, though. The changes we seek will never happen without a dramatic restructuring of our systems, including curriculum, assessments, professional development, student scheduling, teacher autonomy, and community partnerships that are designed to be much more intentional and devout around learning for all kids. These changes will be heavy lifts for all of us, for leading schools in the new century will require the following to become the new normal and a way of work:

Teacher Leadership

No matter what we do to improve our schools and school districts, teachers will lead the way. They are the lifeblood of our industry. In fact, it is sadly ironic to find teachers in most schools and school districts toiling away in obscurity while school principals, district directors, and superintendents make tough instructional decisions.

Yes, the influence of school principals is profound and their roles will continue to shift and expand. Still, no school or school district in the next generation will have widespread and lasting success without genuine teacher leadership. This will require districts to establish committees or boards of directors of some type that include teachers directing the work of teaching and learning. The best school districts will figure this out. They will empower their employees to lead, because if they do not, they will risk losing them to other districts or other professions.

Student Leadership

There is simply too much research and too much common sense to not afford students ample opportunities to collaborate and lead. Whether we call them learning communities, social networks, or something else, these planned opportunities for deep discussion among students must be built into our school schedules in some form or fashion. This may include time for students to team and collaborate without direction and instruction from a teacher. Yes, students need professional learning community time (or professional learning networks) too.

Professionalism/Self-Governance

The education industry must come to grips with the shortcomings of its professional developmenyt, credentialing, and appraisal models. None of them work well enough at present to get us where we need to be. Whatever they become, our solutions must involve higher degrees of professionalism and self-governance on behalf of teachers. Though it is incumbent upon the industry to identify its most struggling and most effective teachers, the time and energy spent on our current appraisal systems cannot be sustained.

The same is true for the tired professional development models in place in many school districts. Neither provide a commensurate return on investment. The same degree of voice, choice, and ownership of learning that we wish for our students must be afforded our teachers. This will raise the stakes, not lower them. It will put great pressure on our teaching profession and union leaders to invest in high-fidelity, high-accountability models by which rich instruction becomes the norm and poor instruction is rooted out.

Curriculum Shifts/Twenty-First-Century Skills

We are never going to inspire, engage, and motivate children if they view their subjects and lessons as disconnected or even random. We must identify the key skills and concepts that students must master and then ensure that we have viable, relatable curricula that overlap subject areas, even if that means covering less material than we do now. This includes cross-training among teachers of various grades and subjects.

A key readiness measure for students in the next century will be their ability to communicate effectively, solve complex problems, think creatively, innovate, pitch their ideas to others, and accept critical feedback. We must find ways to intentionally integrate these twenty-first-century skills into our lessons. Some content knowledge (names, dates, places) will be replaced by soft skills like navigating our communities and workplaces, building authentic relationships, and developing our personal brands.

Flexible Scheduling/Inductive Learning

Schools must be designed around each student's needs, including flexible school days and alternative learning environments. There will be very little room in the future for cookie-cutter lessons and assignments. Learning will become greatly inductive, project-based, place-based, and personalized. Assessment will be wide and deep, from informal talks to juried presentations.

While rigorous classroom instruction remains first and foremost, it is prudent that we provide students more time for personal reflection, independent research, and peer-to-peer interaction. In fact, the day may come where we provide students a day off campus (perhaps at a local college, museum, or business) learning in different environments, researching topics of their own choosing, and developing original business ventures.

Student Sabbaticals/Field Experiences

The future of personalized learning may someday lead to deeper, richer curriculum threads that connect lessons to students' lives, passions, and ambitions. This may lead to scheduled "breaks" from school where students have the time (a day or week or month) to take part in deep research activities or longitudinal projects that go far beyond the canned research papers that we find in most schools today. This may include career exploration activities at local tech companies or short stints as docents at local museums.

Some of these field experiences may include young children moving as groups via extended field trips or older students working individually. Of course, this is not to suggest that these longer breaks from school will occur at home unsupervised. Such opportunities could be supervised off campus with greater participation from our community partners or through planned teacher sabbaticals.

Volunteerism/Activism

The future of our schools will certainly be connected to the promising practices occurring now in revitalizing our neighborhoods and building sustainable communities. This will require our schools and communities to collaborate in giving students purposeful opportunities to volunteer and support their neighbors. These partnerships can provide our students with rich lessons in self-respect, empathy, and pride through community activism and citizenship.

A richer, more meaningful brand of volunteerism will go a long way in helping our young people view community involvement as something they *want* to do and *should* do and not as something they are *compelled* to do as a means of accumulating the community service hours required for school clubs or scholarship applications.

Of course, none of these ideas alone will rid us of our struggles. Still, they are a start. They are part of a set of workable solutions designed to make learning more engaging and relevant for children. In the end, going to school should be fascinating for kids. As much as it can be, learning should involve a series of experiences that are transcendent, even sublime. We need less of:

"The teachers made me do it." And we need more of: "Wow, I discovered something new today," or "I found something out about myself, about what I stand for, and I plan to do something about it."

To this end, many promising trends are emerging across the globe. In 2018, the Ministry of Education in Singapore announced to great fanfare that the country is shifting from a highly structured, highly competitive school system designed to rank and order children to something much more personal than that, with an ambitious plan to graduate children who are highly skilled, but also creatively minded and well-rounded. This dramatic shift includes an emphasis on applied learning and social development and a lesser focus on things like class rankings. The system redesign is scheduled to be fully in place by 2023 (Wood, 2018).

We find similar changes arriving in Finland, a long-standing leader in innovative practices. The country has scrapped traditional school subjects for a multidisciplinary approach that it calls "phenomenon-based" teaching. In essence, Finland is taking a thematic approach by teaching content and skills though broader topics like climate change and community building.

In the United States, innovation is afoot across many states. In California, the whole-child education movement and Linked Learning initiative are creative experiments that are pushing our industry toward highly relevant learning experiences. Though some of these ideas may not succeed, the lessons we learn will push us further toward highly competitive, highly engaging public schools.

Practitioners in the field must be the ones to shape what this change looks like, and that will require us to step back a moment from the mandates and pressures of the next round of state assessments. It will require us to put off filling out the next form that someone just emailed to us and delay the next school visit from the district office staff. Finding the time to do this work is just the beginning. Still, we must get started because a backlash from the public is coming soon, and it will be swift.

REALITY CHECK: A LITTLE TOUGH LOVE

Before we go any further in defining what these someday schools might look like, let us chug back a dose of reality. In fact, let us consider a couple of strong statements that are provided at some risk that you may find this commentary to be untimely or even treasonous. Still, here we go: The idea that schools today do not have the freedom to be creative is simply not true.

The notion that our state and district mandates are so severe and the accountability measures so suffocating that principals cannot lead their schools to greatness is also not true. The same can be said for district leaders who make the same complaints. The concern that teaching to more rigorous standards (e.g., to the Common Core) and requiring students to take standardized tests has sucked all the creative control out of schools is equally not true. Some of these statements may play well politically, but they do not match reality in many cases.

For those who disagree, you might take a moment to tour some of our nation's top schools and sit in a minute among our strongest teachers, each one of them performing at exceptional levels in spite of the mandates handed down in recent years. Of course, we can certainly agree that these new mandates have made instructional creativity, program innovation, and flexible scheduling harder than they need to be. We can also agree that we would do well as a nation to back off some of the top-down accountability measures that have led to the perceptions stated above and the imperfect notion that all children are the same.

These difficult matters need to be brought forward for debate not because they are easy, but because they are hard (with all due respect to President Kennedy's inspiring quote). They are broached at this point in the text because the innovations that we seek will arrive (or not) because of practitioners like you, and we owe it to each other to get it right. In fact, it is the responsibility of practitioners and theoreticians alike to ponder what is possible in our schools and to push us to be better tomorrow, even to the point of thoughtful debate and disagreement.

In fact, we have been through this before in our history, and we have made some strides. To provide a glimmer of hope that what is possible is possible, even probable, let us go back twenty or thirty years ago and celebrate how far we have come as an industry. Let us be reminded how much better we are now at planning rigorous lessons, inspiring higher-order questions, and requiring a greater distribution of student responses.

This growth in instructional best practices is evident among our teachers, but also among our leaders. Our school principals and assistant principals are much better equipped today than ever before in observing teachers, providing meaningful feedback, reviewing academic data, and making instructional decisions around facilities, scheduling, hiring, and professional development. We have a long way to go (we always do), but don't ever buy into the notion that we have not made some significant strides. That is why the industry may be ready to go all in.

As with all dramatic shifts in our schools, we cannot afford to tinker around the edges. We must drill deep into the core of our industry—teaching and learning. That must begin with a review of our current standards and curricula to ensure they are meeting the needs of our kids. The call for much broader twenty-first-century skills has grown louder, though most schools have been slow to embed them in any meaningful way. Yes, the future demands that our students remain highly literate in reading and math, but are also competent in requisite "soft skills" like flexibility and creativity.

Working with their business partners, district curriculum teams will have to agree on which of these new-century skills and competencies we want our students to master, and that work can begin right now. No matter what we decide, our curricula and lessons must keep pace with these changes.

Student work must become more personalized and outcomes must move beyond the current definition of *achievement* as those things measured on standardized assessments. In the new century, achievement will be characterized to a greater degree by the academic skills required to thrive in the real world, along with a blend of social constructs like pride, agility, and even dignity.

WHAT SCHOOLS COULD BE: A PATH TO SELF-ACTUALIZATION

It is not only accurate to say that our industry has evolved and improved over the past decades but also true that a book like this one would not have been possible if not for that improvement. We were simply not ready twenty years ago to implement many of the approaches discussed in this text, just as many of the ideas suggested here will be trumped by even more innovative solutions from our next-generation educators. What will not change is that our success in implementing more creative and systemic approaches will depend (as always) on the confidence and command of great leaders and (yes) in balance with state and national mandates that are ever-changing and unpredictable.

The good news is that the future of our industry is arriving fast under titles like "personalized learning," "project-based learning," "discovery learning," and related concepts like "competency-based progression" and "culturally relevant pedagogy." Whatever we name things in the future, our customers will demand immediate access to content and more control over their learning pathways and timelines. Our students and their parents will demand to be heard, to have a seat at the table, and they are not wrong. They will require of us a system that makes each child's path unique within learning encounters that are dynamic and diverse.

If we can create such experiences in our schools, our leaders will no longer be fixated solely on pedantic tasks like getting kids to pass this class or that one and checking off graduation requirements. Instead, they will be lead learners of creative schools where all children meet minimum expectancies easily and where students arrive each day less focused on passing grades and more immersed in a marketplace of ideas, enterprise, and debate, where civility and citizenship are encouraged, and where struggle and resiliency are tested as a way of inspiring resourcefulness and even wisdom.

This yin and yang of hard and soft skills that our students must master requires us to review what we know about how children learn from decades of social science research in fields that range from child psychology to sociology and ecology. In education, that work cannot begin without a dedicated review of what we know from giants like Abraham Maslow (and others), who had it right all along in pushing our experiences beyond basic life skills toward the grander desires of self-actualization.

Whether we call this ultimate prize of the human condition "wisdom" or "enlightenment" or something else, our common desire to reach a deep level of understanding and consciousness is found within each of us. In the simplest of terms, this is where our schools and school systems have gone astray. This is where we have lost the soul of the system.

There are reports that something is amiss. While students in the United States and around the world continue to get smarter with each generation based on intelligence (IQ) testing, the same trend is not found for things like creativity and ingenuity. In fact, a recent study of 300,000 scores from children on the Torrance Tests of Creative Thinking (TTCT) found that scores for American children increased each year (just like IQ) until about 1990. Since then, creativity scores have declined steadily. In a related finding, a poll of 1,500 CEOs identified creativity as being the top leadership competency required for the next century (Bronson and Merryman, 2010).

Engagement survey after engagement survey tells us that students are craving things like free expression, debate, discovery, and purpose. Interestingly, when our students report that they don't find school relevant, it is not so much the practical application of the material they are talking about (like writing a resume). They are complaining about a lack of appreciation or social connection or even spiritual awakening.

We should all be reminded that our students are not coming to school only to learn facts and figures. Like the rest of us, they seek to be inspired. They come to us escaping the struggles of their families and neighborhoods, even among those students who live in relatively stable homes. They arrive most days searching for something much grander than we offer presently. Far too often, they graduate (or drop out) never having found it.

Students cannot always articulate what they feel, but they are trying to tell us that their interactions in school with our curriculum, materials, and lessons are too often rote and routine. They describe their discussions in school as disconnected and passionless. They find little alignment among the subjects we make them take and no pathway toward the wisdom and self-actualization that they seek.

This is why it is long past time for a dedicated repurposing of our curriculum. If such a thing were in place, our science teachers would not be concerned only with science. Subjects and lessons and standards would be overlapping and meaningful. Teachers would encourage student enterprise and community activism. Teachers too would find more meaning in their work, breathing energy and passion from their interactions with students and their colleagues.

In fact, the role of every person in every school would gain meaning by contributing to a school system that does not rest until it helps all students find their passions and reach their self-actualized goals. To begin this work, we must review the prize of self-actualization as Maslow envisioned it. His work is presented under four related outcomes that may help educators and parents better understand what is being suggested:

1. Self-awareness
2. Self-esteem
3. Self-efficacy
4. Self-reliance

We should be clear that there is nothing magical about these four terms, and there is no order to them. One could be easily discarded for another. They are provided only as related outcomes (and threads for discussion) to bind and orient our work. If nothing else, they are offered as a way of proclaiming from the start that we have set the bar far too low for too many years. In fact, our collective reflection around this work may provide us insight into the scourge of deficit thinking evident throughout our industry.

Though we can agree that the emotional security of our children is foundational to their successes (see Maslow's bottom rungs), we have to wonder if all the energy we spend setting up systems to keep our children emotionally safe has kept us from tending to their deeper needs like belonging, self-worth, passion, and pride (see Maslow's higher rungs). To better understand this dichotomy, it is time to dig deeper into the psychology of human development and ambition.

We will keep a constant eye on Maslow's hierarchy as it provides the genius that grounds our work and inspires the graphic provided (figure 4.2). It should be noted that the Learner Wheel graphic is presented only as a starting point to stir discussion about what we teach our children. In keeping with Maslow's hierarchy, the wheel is designed to attend firstly to each student's human needs and desires and secondly to his or her academic ones.

MASLOW WHISPERERS: WHAT THE HIERARCHY IS REALLY TELLING US

Maslow's hierarchy is to educators what girth is to sumo wrestlers—far-reaching and essential. For years, we have planned our training of new teachers in part around his famous pyramid model. Somewhat surprisingly, our focus has been almost exclusively on the bottom rungs. That is where Maslow famously claims that no real learning or human advancement can come without the learner feeling first safe and loved. As any educator will tell you, there is nothing more foundational than that.

Still, it is fair to consider whether this base rung of the hierarchy is also where our deficit thinking creeps in, as we often view students as the goofy, silly, rebellious children they are and not as the extraordinary, transcendent figures they can someday be. For whatever reason, scant attention has been paid across our industry to the top layers of Maslow's model, with all due respect to those of us who believe we are helping kids by loving them to death.

In fact, if we go back to the set of belief statements set forth in chapter 2, we will find that one of the key tenets of leading with an instructional soul is the honest, unwavering claim that all children can learn at very, very high levels. No child is exempt from exceptionalism. What does this mean for us? What are the consequences at stake for our industry?

It means that many of the students who are underperforming in our schools are doing so because the systems we have established are not pushing them to greater heights. It means that some students are underperforming not because of something they have done (or not done), but because of what we have done in designing their schools, curriculum, and lessons.

For those who may liken these ideas to psychological gobbledygook, let us trot out a practical example at this time. Let us try to imagine what our schools would be like if they were not centered around distinct subjects but around lessons in literacy and numeracy that are connected to life skills like empathy and dignity or even social and economic issues like water quality or energy independence. *How many windmills do we need for wind energy to be successful? Is there a cost in giving up that much land? What are the alternatives in broadening our energy landscape?*

In fact, for many schools and districts, this type of work is not that far afield. We have tinkered with and tweaked ideas like this for years, though we have little to show for it. As for the traditionalists who say that we must retain our distinct academic disciplines as we now have them, can we at least request that those disciplines be better aligned for students of the next century?

If Maslow were here, he would tell us that every human being can aspire to self-actualization (though it is rare to accomplish it) and that our studies should push us beyond things like safety and skill-building. In recording his observations, Maslow went so far as to study and name those who he believed reached the pinnacle of self-actualization during their lifetimes, including Albert Einstein and Abraham Lincoln. While most of us will never reach those levels of notoriety, our schools would be wise to consider how to establish systems that push students to loftier heights of academic confidence and personal clarity. Anything less feels sadly unambitious.

In summarizing his studies of Maslow's work, popular writer-researcher David Sze compiled twelve characteristics of self-actualized adults (figure 4.1) that may help us contextualize our work as teachers of children. In fact, if we parcel out these characteristics in just the right manner, we might be able to establish curriculum frameworks and lessons designed to impart these competencies upon our children. This is certainly an ambitious endeavor in light of all the other demands we have before us. Still, it provides us with refreshing possibilities to explore in creating more soulful experiences for our learners.

KEY DRIVER 3: REPURPOSE SCHOOL CURRICULUM

Designing a pathway for young adults to have efficient and equitable routes to success will require curriculum shifts that are responsive to the new age. The Learner Wheel (figure 4.2) attempts to capture such shifts by presenting the path that a typical learner takes toward self-actualization. The graphic is provided not as a finished product but as an evolving idea, especially knowing that demands on instruction will continue to change and because Maslow tells us that a person's route is not always linear. It is presented like any other graphic organizer in helping us view complex concepts in simpler forms and, as systems thinkers, to see the connections in our work.

What we all want for our children and what the future demands of us as educators is that we graduate students as highly articulate and productive citizens. In getting us closer to that reality, the concepts presented within the wheel are starting points for aligning our curricula, lessons, and assessments. They also underpin our work as we consider a full overhaul of critical systems such as teacher planning and training, leadership development, family involvement, and community connections.

The wheel establishes a continuum of skills that a student might master in reaching the outcomes of self-awareness, self-esteem, self-efficacy, and self-reliance. These four conditions of consciousness should be viewed as nearly synonymous and purposely overlapping. The concepts and related terms are presented as a circle but do not have to be seen that way, since viewing them as a list or along a number line would be just as effective. The only caution here is presenting them as a pyramid as no hierarchy is required nor suggested in this text. Maslow has already provided that for us.

In fact, the only attempt at structure within the wheel is the placement of a few ideas closer to the center of the circle. If we focus our eyes there, we find terms that are common antecedents that students typically master on their way to learning higher-order abilities over time. We should be quick to note

Maslow's Hierarchy / Key Characteristics of Self-Actualized Adults

1. **They embrace the unknown and the ambiguous.**
   They are not threatened or afraid of it.
2. **They accept themselves, together with all of their flaws.**
   They perceive themselves as they are, and not what they would prefer to be.
3. **They prioritize and enjoy the journey, not just the destination.**
   They regard as ends those experiences that are, for other people, only means.
4. **They are inherently unconventional, though they do not seek to shock or disturb.**
   They accept the world of people that they do not understand nor approve of.
5. **They are motivated by growth, not by the satisfaction of needs.**
   They are focused on personal growth.
6. **They share deep relationships with a few, but also feel identification and affection toward the entire human race.**
   They have deeper and more profound interpersonal relationships than any other adults.
7. **They are not troubled by the small things.**
   They focus on the big picture.
8. **They are grateful.**
   They do not take their blessings for granted.
   They maintain a fresh sense of wonder toward the universe.
9. **They are humble.**
   They are well aware of how little they know in comparison with what could be known, and what is known by others.
10. **They resist enculturation.**
    They do not allow themselves to be passively molded by culture.
    They deliberate and make their own decisions.
11. **They are not perfect.**
    They recognize that there are people who are good, even great,
    and yet the same people can be boring, irritating, petulant, selfish, angry, or depressed.
12. **They have purpose.**
    They have some mission in life, some task to fulfill.
    They have some problem outside themselves that enlists much of their energies.

Figure 4.1. Maslow's Hierarchy/Key Characteristics of Self-Actualized Adults
Note: Figure is an adaptation originally published as "Maslow: The 12 Characteristics of a Self-Actualized Person" (Sze, 2017). *Source:* David Sze, 2017, "Maslow: The 12 Characteristics of a Self-Actualized Person," Life (blog), *Huffington Post*, December 6, 2017, www.huffpost.com/entry/maslow-the-12-characteris_n_7836836 (accessed March 3, 2019).

that the terms closer to the center are basic skills and simple social constructs like *caring* and *civility* that we already teach in school.

A Path to Self-Actualization

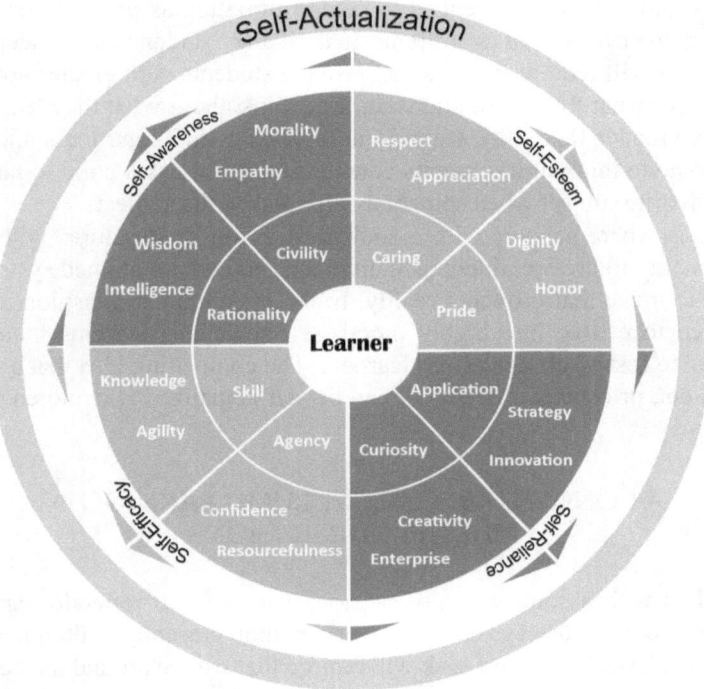

Figure 4.2. Systems/Learner Wheel

Of course, in keeping with what we know from extant brain research, children are quite different and can learn at different rates. For this reason, the wheel is not meant to imply that everyone starts at the same place, where simpler concepts must be mastered before continuing to the next. For example, a school could encourage curiosity (a simple concept, easy to incorporate) through a series of entrepreneurial activities that require students to show creativity and enterprise (complex concepts, not so easy to do). This is where systems come in.

We know that most students will not reach the highest levels of awareness and metacognition unless and until our lessons and outcomes aspire to such things. Inductive pedagogy is one such option that may open up new opportunities worth exploring. Some schools are already experimenting with inductive approaches (learning through discovery) and away from deductive learning (learning from the teacher). These new approaches help us to view content as subjective and malleable, where facts and truth are worthy of discussion.

In this type of learning environment, students own the content (not the teacher). Students are challenged to take information as provided or uncovered and then rework it or reframe it until they understand it deeply. Of course, this will require systems that provide students with greater voice and choice over what they learn and what they think about what they learn. This includes broader flexibility around the topics we study and the subjects we take. Come to think of it, it seems counterintuitive to ask a child to name his or her favorite subject when somebody else picked the subjects.

This is where schools with a soul must establish structures with fierce intentionality to grow children as individuals, and where aligned systems are created to make that growth a reality. In the most dramatic fashion, schools will need to evolve into highly moral, self-actualized systems themselves designed to foster self-actualized learners. The compelling idea that a school, department, or central office itself can be self-actualized is explored in later chapters.

A CONCENTRIC CURRICULUM: LEARNING IN MULTIPLE DIMENSIONS

As leaders with a soul, we must be honest in our self-reflection and self-criticism because the systems we work within presently will not change without us. The changes we seek will require that we see around the bend and that we propose solutions that to some may seem like science fiction. The reason for this is obvious. We only know what we know, and there is no need to apologize for that.

This is the very reason why a young middle school principal recently lamented that he was not bringing an exciting, experiential learning concept to his school because it didn't fit neatly into his school's seven-period schedule. These are the limits that most of us place on ourselves, in large part because of the system someone placed us in.

It is the same reason why any intelligent person can easily explain three-dimensional objects to a friend but cannot fathom what that same object might look like if it were in four dimensions. As leaders, we must prepare ourselves for such new realities, and we have got to know that shifting our thinking will be frustrating at times.

The aspirational framework proposed via this chapter is not linear, and that is hard to imagine for some. This concept is multidimensional. It is not reading or math or science. It is not writing or public speaking or character education. It isn't even coding or mastering the Microsoft Office Suite. Even more troubling, it isn't first period or second period or this teacher or that one. The reality of this new type of schooling takes us to a multidimensional space where students are learning more than one thing simultaneously and organically. If you prefer, it is a place where one learning experience leads to multiple outcomes, where singular things create multiple shadows.

For purposes of this text, we will refer to this new curriculum reality as a concentric curriculum, one that is both highly ethereal and highly scaffolded in building student competencies for tackling whatever life brings their way. This work is not as far-fetched as it may seem, as many creative interpretations are underway right now in forward-thinking school districts and global think tanks. One place to start is by checking out the fascinating work happening at the Center for Curriculum Redesign and its books and articles on four-dimensional education.

In giving us a historical perspective of dramatic curriculum shifts, we might also review the notes we took in college on the writings of philosopher and futurist John Dewey. It is so easy to look back now and view his writings as old-school wisdoms or truisms, though we should keep in mind that Dewey was pushing educational reforms when there was little or no science to back up his claims.

In his famous manuscript *Democracy and Education* (2004 [1916]), Dewey describes what he considers one of the key outcomes of any successful school or system—teaching students how to learn. There is where he introduces us to the concept of "plasticity":

> This is something quite different from the plasticity of putty or wax. It is not a capacity to take on change of form in accord with external pressure. It lies near the pliable elasticity by which some persons take on the color of their surroundings while retaining their own bent. But it is something deeper than this. It is essentially the ability to learn from experience; the power to retain from one experience something which is of avail in coping with the difficulties of a later situation. This means power to modify actions on the basis of the results of prior experiences, the power to develop dispositions. Without it, the acquisition of habits is impossible. (pp. 42–43)

This kind of thinking is one of the reasons why Dewey was not a big fan of vocational education in its original conception, as a way of tracking students into a job. You may disagree, but he did not view skill-building as the aim of schooling. He found it far more valuable for students to learn about themselves, about the way they learn, and about the habits that would carry them through whatever life presented them.

This thinking is akin to the commentary we hear today about twenty-first-century skills as those that transfer from job to job. To be clear, the demands of the job market will always require schools to teach hard skills (from cooking to computer repair), though any modern curricula must provide these things alongside transferable soft skills.

Let's look at three easy examples of skills that could be folded into any lesson within any subject in getting us closer to an aligned, concentric curriculum.

- *Adaptability.* A multidimensional curriculum does not simply require that our teachers *adapt* their lessons to meet the needs and interests of the students in their classes. It also challenges us to create opportunities for children to actually learn what it means to *adapt* to their surroundings, from subject matter they have not yet seen to problems they have not yet faced.

  While some love the idea that students are learning crafts such as carpentry, Dewey would prefer that we use classes like carpentry to teach students to be problem-solvers (engineers if you will). Why? Because while it is great to learn how to measure twice and cut once as a carpenter, it is even more important to know how to use that skill in tackling problems that work and life will present our students across their lifetimes. Again, a balance of hard and soft skills will be critical.
- *Flexibility.* We know quite well that the children who went to school way back in the twentieth century and before were likely to find employment doing one thing. Those students became doctors or dentists, tradesmen or craftsmen, farmers or factory workers. A subtle few advanced to college and fewer still joined the high society that we know of as professors, politicians, scientists, and social entrepreneurs. The old-century world, the one where things change slowly, has been relegated to the history books.

  Even if it is true that someone can still find work doing one thing (being a police officer, for example) it is nearly impossible to advance in any career or change careers unless we find ways to redefine ourselves, to appreciate the perspectives of others, and to embrace changes in technology, science, and public policy. Like adaptability, it is not enough for our teachers to be flexible in how they offer up their lessons; it is critical that the lessons themselves be designed to teach students the art of flexibility.
- *Resiliency.* Teaching children within a student-centered framework requires us to stand by each child all the way to the end, to be partners in their struggle, and to facilitate their growth even when the cycle of failure kicks in. The resiliency required of educators (and all adults) to be successful in the workplace is a skill that young people need to learn in school, especially for those striving to rise above lives of poverty, neglect, and prejudice.

  A great deal of research and dialogue on the topics of resiliency and grit as key factors for success have made their way into our industry, and that may spark new ideas in molding these skills within our children. There is little reason for students to be experts in math and science standards if they are not learning as well to be determined and resilient young adults.

In his extensive writings on school reform, Dewey implored his colleagues in education to provide students the skills and habits of learning they would need to take on the challenges of work and life. Or as Dewey (2004 [1916]) described the learner: "He learns to learn" (p. 44).

The latest research on how we "learn to learn" comes under titles like "self-efficacy," and this is described in the current literature as more than a belief in one's self. True self-efficacy requires that our confidence in ourselves be tied to a belief that we can control our futures, our own destinies. This is more than simple optimism. It is operational self-actualization, for we have designed the systems required to get us there.

SCHOOL IS ABOUT THEM, NOT US

Installing bold new systems for a new age will recenter our work and remind us that students must be at the core of our endeavors, not accountability measures or standards. If we are accountability-focused, we will push students to meet only those requirements as measured by the state (and little else). In fact, we do this now. In reality, we don't focus on things like soft skills, because no one measures them. We don't push children to the heights of self-actualization, because no one is holding us accountable for doing it.

If we are standards-focused, we will put our energies behind getting the standards in front of students at all costs (even at the expense of engagement). This is tempting, but fleeting. While students are pushed to master more complex tasks, schools are forced to scale back on assignments and projects designed to inspire ingenuity and creative expression. In fact, the cracks in the standards movement are already showing.

On the contrary, if we design systems that are student-focused, we are pushed to conceive of schools where students thrive at all costs, where learning (not teaching) is our nucleus, where any child who underperforms is seen as unacceptable (even unfathomable). As we unpack all of this as an industry, we will wrestle over how to break free from the tired routine of separating skills and standards into subjects that have no common thread, a relic that must be placed among the dusty books in our garages. In doing so, we will uncover a richer, integrated curricula unlike anything we have seen before.

We will empower teachers to reclaim ownership of lessons that are not cookie-cutter but focused on what each child needs, and we will give greater agency over to students in discovering their own voices and passions. No matter what results, these debates will help us wrest back control of our schools, burst the shackles of departmentalization and bureaucracy, and breathe in the fresh air of academic freedom.

Chapter Five

The Possibilities of Community

For children everywhere, the path of adolescence is paved hard by experience. Along the way, each child learns the critical life lessons and survival skills that he or she needs to succeed in a sometimes harsh, unforgiving world. As children learn, they falter a little, fail some, learn new skills, falter again, and then learn some more. All the while, they adapt and mature (as we all do) along a continuum of experiences that does not vary much from child to child no matter where we grow up in the world. Though our conditions may differ vastly, our responses do not.

If all goes well, we advance and succeed (some more than others). Our survival skills become routines supported by increasingly deeper levels of knowledge, richer degrees of metacognition, and a clearer understanding of ourselves and the world around us. All of this learning might be termed "wisdom" or "enlightenment." If we add in a deeper sense of morality, we might begin to describe what we are experiencing as "self-actualization" or even "spirituality."

It is clear that our schools and school districts play a critical role in developing (or not) these self-actualizing behaviors in children. The point has been made that redefining our vision with greater singularity within schools could inspire something profound by expecting much more of our children and ourselves than we do now. This new way of doing business will require an elevated response from the system itself, an ethereal mix of curricula and lessons and collaboration designed to produce highly competent and confident young adults who are aware of their place in the world and their purpose in it.

Truth be told, these rich experiences will never happen in schools alone. Aspiring to such lofty heights for learning will require a wider reach for school systems and grander expectations around school-community partnerships. Such changes cannot occur in schools as they are presently constructed nor in communities that see their local schools as the places they drop their kids off in the morning and pick them up in the afternoon, kind of like getting an oil change.

Though we might know and trust our mechanics, we really have no idea what they're doing once we hand over the keys. If the repair requires something complex like a new transmission, we pretend to understand what we are hearing as the mechanic stumbles on about crankshafts and couplings and standards and factoring and fluency. "Stop right there. You lost me. Just tell me when it will be ready, and I'll be back to pick it up."

PARALLEL SOLUTIONS: EVOLVE AND EMPOWER

So what expectations should the system have for itself in orchestrating such profound changes, and what expectations might those outside the system (the community, for example) have for us while such changes are underway? The answers might surprise you but, in the end, will cause each of us a lot less frustration as we suffer the slow march of change. Let's consider two parallel responses that school districts can put into play immediately:

Evolve: Allow the System to Evolve Naturally

As evidenced by changes observed across ecosystems, the pace of evolution (or rate of change) can be painfully slow. Systems can take lifetimes to evolve into something new and interesting, a natural pace that can be frustrating to the observer but comfortable for the system itself. Of course, this is not always the case. A system can also change dramatically, even overnight.

We are all aware of systems that have experienced radical makeovers that are born out of chaos (a fire in the wilderness) or revolution (the takeover of a business by a trendy newcomer). Of course, such revolutionary ventures are risky and sometimes fail. For this reason, the system will always fight against revolutionary change at all costs.

To combat this push back, Senge (1990) makes the case for a just-right approach that he calls the "optimal rate of growth" so that change is manageable and doesn't overwhelm the system. "The optimal rate is far less than the fastest possible growth. When growth becomes excessive—as it does in cancer—the system itself will seek to compensate by slowing down; perhaps putting the organization's survival at risk in the process" (p. 62).

As hard as it is for visionaries to admit, the system must grow at a pace that will ensure its survival. Any effort to the contrary will force the system into a highly defensive posture, and it will fight back aggressively. No system will put its survival at risk. In the education industry, this is evident in the public school system's unholy alliance with charter schools and its passive aggressive attacks on those who offer solutions that include private school vouchers or public-private partnerships.

The sometimes visceral defense put forth by superintendents, teachers unions, and other insiders whenever someone suggests a new way to do schooling via charter or private schools is a screaming example of the system's survival instincts. This is not to say that the fears expressed are not real, but they are born out of a deep socio-psychological framework that all human beings have to avoid the discomforts of change and to assign structure to chaos.

This text will stay clear of the political debates on the merits of charter schools, but the cry for radical changes to public school education that we hear from politicians, parents, and pundits is real and our defensiveness is as well. No matter the fixes that are proposed, some degree of caution is prudent as there is risk in moving too quickly. This is probably why the world is not managed by dreamers. Though the technological and curricular advancements in schools today are prodding at best, school systems are improving, and maintaining that trajectory will be critical.

As for the dreamers, they will have to be patient. The education industry is full of visionaries and that is a good thing. In fact, many of us wish to be counted among them. They are eager to blog and post about bold ideas with great gusto. The most boisterous in the industry are calling for immediate change (revolution) over slow growth (evolution). Still, even the radicals among us know that most people do not have the stomach for it. Even the revolutionaries tarry on each day with the wisdom of seasoned pragmatists, though reluctant ones at best.

Empower: Leverage the System to Our Advantage

Since the system is more comfortable evolving slowly, leaders must find ways to work with the system, through the system, or around the system to avoid the frustration that comes with waiting around so long that no one cares anymore. Yes, we must be patient and progressive at the same time. School districts cannot count on slow-and-steady growth, lest we all wake up one day and find our current schools are irrelevant or extinct.

In an age where innovation is measured in months and not years, schools cannot simply wait around. We must be on the lookout now for the critical changes needed to keep us in the game. This is the crisis at hand that school leaders do not always see. This is where true soul-searching is required if we are to become authentic partners with our teachers, students, parents, and communities.

Substantive changes within systems can always be traced to single points, though we often don't notice them at the time. Systems will not change without defining moments, without a game changer. This can be a person or an event (no matter how small) that pushes the system slightly off course and, in the end, toward a new destination that it never before thought possible.

In systems theory, this is called a leverage point. Meadows (2008) describes it as "embedded in legend: the silver bullet, the trimtab; the miracle cure; the secret passage; the magic password; the single hero who turns the tide of history; the nearly effortless way to cut through or leap over huge obstacles" (p. 145).

In the education industry, our leverage point must arrive soon. In fact, the thing we are seeking may be right in front of us if we only knew how to leverage it. It might be authentic parent involvement; it might be greater teacher leadership and autonomy; it might be personalized or project-based learning. It may be something we have not yet defined. Whatever it is, leaders need to be on the lookout for it, and some brave souls will need to embrace it fully to push the industry off its present course. Finding it will require leaders to remain alert because leverage points are not always so obvious and frequently are not intuitive.

A POSSIBLE LEVERAGE POINT: WIDENING THE SYSTEM

One way to envision such a shift in the industry is to view our local communities not as tangential to our success but as central to the school system itself. The community as the system. The school building as the centrifuge for learning, as the nucleus. In doing so, communities could support deeper learning by integrating local experiences into district curriculum, bringing relevancy and context to the static facts and figures offered in school. Schools could serve as hubs for providing educational services to the community, as agents for fostering community dialogue, and as centers for family wellness and socio-emotional health.

In designing what this looks like, we must examine closely the lessons we have learned from the community school models across the country. We have learned much from these experiments regarding social services that we can offer and business partnerships we can cultivate. We have also witnessed the push and pull from the competing definitions that leaders have for school-community partnerships. Much of the work in our community schools has centered on after-school programs for students and families and community access to school facilities.

Though these are positive steps, it is time to push much further in considering models that are not so much about bringing community services to the school site but as opportunities to rebrand our communities as our classrooms. Once again, we would do well to retrace the thinking of John Dewey and others who pushed for these innovations as early as the 1800s. He joined the progressive thinkers of the time in rallying against schools and lessons that were uncoupled from their neighboring communities. He saw them as one in the same, an idea referred to at that time as "school extension."

Many of the radical notions expressed in those days continue to influence current research and thinking on community schooling. In keeping with the themes of this text, it is paramount that school districts widen their view of community-school partnerships if we are ever to keep our promise to develop the whole child and inspire a more soulful upbringing.

For those who see all of this as pushing the system a bit too far, it may be helpful to reflect upon the exhilarating changes witnessed by the travel industry and many others over the past decades. In the world that our grandparents grew up in, a travel agency was a building they visited in planning an itinerary and booking reservations for hotels, cruises, and air travel. Of course, those days are hardly recognizable. Though some travel agencies still exist, any family from anywhere can book their entire vacation without the help of an agent through a series of aligned, online resources.

Many of the things we take for granted today did not exist the day we were born. Of course, all of this is available to us because someone not so long ago decided to study, research, and pilot how to make life easier to plan and execute. As a result, the travel industry is no longer a building. It is no longer an appointment with an agent. It is no longer brochures and maps and postcards. That was so 1980s. Now, the travel industry is an app.

In truth, the industry has evolved to such a degree that the consumer may find it difficult to sort out where travel planning ends and actual traveling begins. Even when our hotel reservations are made and our plane tickets are purchased, these same online sites can assist us in locating great restaurants, navigating city streets, and sharing our experiences with friends via social media. Somewhere along the way, the travel industry found its leverage point, and it has not been the same since.

Of course, innovations such as these require aspiring entrepreneurs who can envision such a thing. With all due respect to travel agents, they would never have designed such a system. In fact, they might have battled these changes at all costs. That's why the industry needed a game changer, someone unafraid to take a few steps toward equitable access, fewer roadblocks, less frustration, and the easiest possible routes for us to spend our money. True empowerment. A travel agency without walls.

The education industry is in dire need of such a transformation. In fact, it may be true that the leverage points we are seeking are available now if we slowed down long enough to look around and catalog the realities before us. And make no mistake. There are consequences if we do not act. If we don't get it right, the schools of today could become the travel agencies of a previous generation. Our schools could become the libraries of a previous era. We could become Kodak.

PLANNED REVOLUTION: GOING ALL IN

Google rocked our world. Its arrival just twenty years ago changed our lives the way the invention of the internet and the telephone did for previous generations. We went to bed one night with volumes of encyclopedias stacked neatly on our bookshelves, and we woke up to instant access to information in a single click. We have seen this time and time again across many industries, from Netflix to Amazon. Tired concepts from one generation give rise to radical innovations that empower consumers in providing them greater control over the information they seek and the decisions they make.

Yes, change can occur just like that. Though great caution is in order, the changes we seek may arrive soon and suddenly. Don't let anyone fool you. In fact, many of the stunning advancements we marvel at today were conceived by those same leaders who grew up flipping through the well-worn pages of dusty encyclopedias, way back when the school year did not begin without new correction tape for our typewriters, when we had nine planets, and we made popcorn on the stove.

In weighing the criticisms of our current school systems, it is fair to ask if the education industry has kept pace with these extraordinary times. In his blockbuster book, *The World Is Flat*, Thomas Friedman (2006) makes the bold claim that a middle-class kid in India has just as much chance of inventing a new product, marketing it, and becoming a worldwide phenomenon as a middle-class kid from middle America. This is another way of saying that if we don't invent better school systems, someone else will.

This is especially difficult to hear when so many in the education industry are open to change but cannot fathom how and when it might happen. The psychology that propels us to innovate is helpful in envisioning a path forward. Let's use the evolution of the typewriter as an example. As we all know, the typewriter was an indispensable tool for families for more than one hundred years. Families loved their typewriters and most purchased new ones every few years in keeping up with the latest tweaks and gadgets, from color ink ribbons to self-correction options.

In fact, we might still be tweaking the typewriter today had someone not decided that we needed something more revolutionary than color ink. Something never before imagined. It is important to remind us that long before the world could summon the idea of a word processor or desktop computer, someone had to decide that making a better typewriter wasn't going to get us where we needed to be.

In pondering a similar leap of faith, it is hard to imagine any successful school model that doesn't include stronger partnerships with our neighborhoods, recreation centers, little leagues, police departments, museums, and city halls. It is equally impossible to consider a seismic shift occurring without passionate involvement from our children and families.

It may help to fast forward this line of thinking by envisioning a day where children are at the center of their communities much more than they are now. This will require a significant shift in our community mindset. In truth, if we gathered all of the little league coaches, business leaders, and city council members into a room right now, most could not tell us what is happening in our reading or social studies classrooms any more than our children could tell them what happens at a city council meeting.

Even among our school families, many have no real sense of what their children are learning in school. Many cannot describe what their sons and daughters know and don't know, save what we tell them via report cards and test scores. In fact, describing our children by their class ranks or grade point averages is like describing our favorite foods by their calorie counts. Somehow we are missing the beauty, the art, the soul.

Whatever partnerships are formed, schools will remain central to the cause. Families and communities will count on us even more, though they will no longer see school as the only place where learning occurs. We owe it to our communities to change the perception of our schools as places where children are separated and sorted, as an uninviting collection of hallways hidden behind fences, as mysterious sites where the adults on the inside are convinced that much is going on while those on the outside are left to wonder what all the commotion is about.

SCHOOLS WITHOUT FENCES: COMMUNITIES IN MOTION

Shifting our mindsets about schools begs an important question about whether or not our communities themselves are child-centered. Let's face it. Our neighborhoods and towns are built primarily to serve adults, from the services provided to the infrastructures in place. A few exceptions are found here or there, including local ballfields and recreation centers. Listening to teenagers complain about a lack of safe and fun things to do on the weekends is all the evidence we need.

As was stated in previous chapters, even schools can be places where the interests of adults come before children. The future will demand that this perception shifts. In fact, what is being suggested here is an approach that really isn't new at all. Not so long ago, there was a time where schools and churches were at the center of their communities (and sometimes within the same building).

Though the separation of church and state remains critical to our democracy, the sense of community we once had in having a common town center or meeting place is now missing. A spirit that once was is now hard to find, in part because there is no such place to gather and no cause to rally around.

This is where our schools can regain their standing, by establishing themselves as hubs for involvement and innovation, as community organizers for raising great children. Strangely, there is something missing in a community when the raising of children is not viewed as a community effort. When it comes to reading, writing, factoring, and fractions, the job of teaching children is left almost entirely to schools in the same way that firefighting is left to the firefighters. *That's not my job. That's why we have teachers. I trust (or not) that they know what they are doing.*

It is simply not common to find strong community involvement in schools. We have heard countless politicians claim that raising children "takes a village" only to see the development of our youth handed over to schools and parents who are rarely on the same page and hardly communicating. Though all parents (yes, *all* parents) care deeply about their children, most feel like they are on their own in raising them. It is the same sentiment that teachers and school leaders relay about schooling. We're doing the best we can, but it feels like we're going it alone.

This is not to suggest that all stakeholders don't share the same concerns. In truth, the community partnerships we devise will be made easier because we are closer in alignment on what we want for our children than some might think. No matter the parent you speak to, the police officer you encounter, or the pastor you visit with, they have similar hopes for our youth. We all want to raise smart, well-mannered children who will someday lead productive lives and pass on those qualities to children of their own.

No matter the words we use to describe them, there are only a few qualities we want for our children. Here are five to consider: maturity, kindness, confidence, ingenuity, wisdom. Those may not be your top five, but they are outcomes that any parent would take for their children. (As the parent of a teenager, I would take even one of them.) More than that, most parents will tell you that the challenge of raising children might be easier if such things were infused into our school lessons and assignments. It is only logical that our youth coaches, government agencies, and local businessmen and women are involved as well.

It is probably worth noting that any suggestion that schools should be welcoming families in instead of keeping folks away is mentioned here in a community-building context, with all due respect to the practical challenges in place. Though this book is centered on visioning a better way for our schools and communities to partner, no one can imagine a day anytime soon where we have open campuses (literally no fences). The metaphor of an inviting school culture is all that is implied.

KEY DRIVER 4: RE-ENGAGE SCHOOL COMMUNITIES

The Community Wheel graphic (figure 5.1) is presented as a companion to the Learner Wheel presented in the previous chapter. Like the Learner Wheel, this one is not created as a finished product but as a draft framework for aligning our thinking about partnerships with local actors and agencies. This is a discussion worth having because schools are seeking fresh ideas for building purposeful community partnerships.

Most school leaders struggle with balancing such things. Throughout the industry, we have not figured out how to manage the enticing but perplexing notion of leveraging parents, mentors, and business partners. The conversations in schools always come down to this unspoken truth: we have no idea what to do with them. Sure, we're happy to have the help, but what on earth

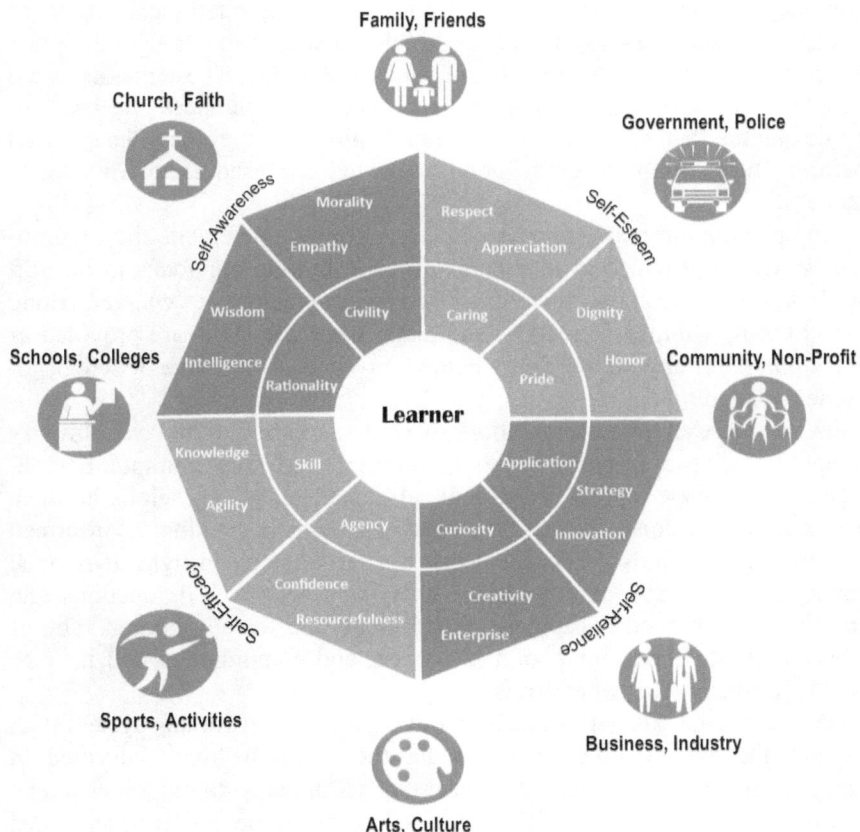

Figure 5.1. Systems/Community Wheel

are we supposed to do with them? They are not educators. They are not trained. So how can they really help our children learn?

In the absence of more substantive options, our stock response is to involve them in mentoring. Mentors are paired with struggling students and asked to focus on simple messages about coming to school, listening to your teachers, and doing your homework. The nationwide movement to bring more mentors into our schools has been tremendously helpful in encouraging kids to stay focused on school success.

In fact, if all kids attended school, listened to their teachers, contributed in class, and did their homework, our children and families would be much better off. To be sure, mentoring is meaningful to children and we never have enough caring folks signing up to help. Even so, a daring but necessary next step is rallying our volunteers and business partners to move from mentor to full-on instructional partner.

Think of it like the challenge we find in our messaging to parents about how they can get involved. As we grasp for something to tell them, we return to the same platitudes about encouraging their children to get a good night's sleep or asking them what they learned in school today. These messages are coupled with an endless parade of parent-teacher conferences and back-to-school nights that have our parents complaining that they have heard it all before. They are left bereft of good ideas and confused as to what really matters.

In updating our messaging around community involvement, the Community Wheel is provided as a place to begin in turning our focus to the soft skills and self-actualizing behaviors discussed in the previous chapter. Along with tutoring children in reading and math, these life skills are provided as entry points for anyone seeking a community impact initiative or school-to-home collaborative.

While these are intriguing notions, we must be careful to not oversimplify things. Creating a system of schools, families, and local communities designed to graduate highly skilled and self-actualized young adults is much easier said than done. In fact, some may question if creating an informed citizenry by anyone's definition is just too far-reaching in light of societal challenges. We have to consider if knowing fractions and functions and sporting an advanced vocabulary is really possible for all children. This is where a comfortable entry point is needed, and communities will have to decide for themselves what that is.

As we debate this, let us remember that a core belief for any system with a soul is that every child can learn and has the right to be highly educated. In fact, we have to wonder why it is that students in many communities attend similar schools in similar neighborhoods, and yet some end with advanced literacy and math skills, while others struggle to master the basic concepts required to graduate.

Though politicians may say otherwise, the difference in learning outcomes cannot be easily explained by saying that some schools are great and others are awful or that some teachers are super and some are lousy. Those inside the system will tell you that the challenges are much more complex than that.

Creating community solutions will require deep introspection, along with discussions of gender, race, poverty, and bias. The community must come to grips with the fact that some students are not as well prepared as others and that we all share in that reality. It is both logical and historically true that whatever we become in life is almost entirely the result of the families who raise us, the friends we surround ourselves with, and the teachers and mentors who give us guidance along the way.

No matter how successful and supportive a school becomes, the children who attend that school are not likely to progress at the same rates if they do not go home to moderately stable environments or surround themselves with strong mentors who keep them safe and focused. The lucky ones who have involved families (no matter the student's socioeconomic status) do much better in school and life than those whose families pay little attention. This is made worse when those same children attend schools that have low expectations, unspoken biases, and underskilled teachers.

Yes, despite our progress, learning is still a lottery. Though it is deeply troubling to admit, it cannot be denied. While we can all point to someone who has overcome family challenges and struggling schools, many children do not. Those who rise above such things remain the exception and not the rule. Creating a better system will require us to fashion a school-community model that increases the chances for students of poverty, for those with uninvolved parents, and for those with underskilled teachers.

This will require community stakeholders, including our mayors and mentors, to be well-versed in what is happening behind the school gates and to invest in their own training so we can move beyond the platitudes and pleasantries ("Work hard. Get a good night's sleep.") in becoming true partners in learning ("Now, sit down here a minute, and let me help you with your homework.").

SELF-ACTUALIZED SYSTEMS: A SCHOOL DISTRICT PRIMER

It is difficult to fathom a fully aligned, community-minded school system when communities and agencies are separated by fences as well. Politics and power are two such barriers that must be breached. In giving structure to the cause, school districts may consider working with local leaders on a community compact of some sort that outlines key factors to student success and which agencies are partnering on which parts. Below are five broad factors to consider:

1. Safety/security
2. Citizenship/activism
3. Literacy/vocabulary
4. Local history/politics
5. Enterprise/creativity

A school-community collaborative on homelessness or recycling is one of many examples. One such project that a school and community partnered on recently was on gardening and nutrition. Most of the neighborhood children had never been to a farm and had never seen a garden. In fact, some had never eaten fresh vegetables. While many schools and neighborhoods have built community gardens, the school in this example went much, much further. First, the school's science curriculum was adapted to align with the broader themes of nutrition and sustainability.

Next, a grower from a local farm volunteered to teach at the school, not as a guest speaker but once a week as the unit instructor. Students spent much of their class time outside tending to the garden and learning about everything from measurement to insects and irrigation. Of course, the students learned about the benefits of fresh foods, sampled many varieties of lettuce and other vegetables, and even took some home to their families.

It should be noted that shared experiences like these can lead to shared resources, including shared faculty and facilities. As easy options, we might consider partnerships between school libraries and community libraries. Or shared athletic facilities. Or shared performance venues. These are things we can envision when we view student success as a community outcome.

Of course, the most stunning advancements in school-community partnerships would arrive if we could unveil some sort of shared ownership of academic content. Within our current model, nearly everything we teach is created and commissioned by schools and teachers, from the materials we use to the lessons we design. It is troubling to find that our students are showing up to class in many schools with little investment in what they are learning. It should be noted that our parents are experiencing the same things.

Let's take a look at what this sounds like to families at a typical open house event: *"Welcome, we are very happy that you're here. I am Mrs. Prescott, your child's language arts teacher. One of our primary tasks this year is to learn to write properly with little to no errors in grammar or mechanics. Specifically, we will be learning how to write in active voice instead of passive voice as this is a skill that most students do not do well . . . etc."* The teacher might go on to explain that an essay will be assigned each week (her choice), what the topics are going to be (her choice), and how the grades will be determined (her choice).

Now, let's take a moment to contrast this example with a message to families that would be quite a bit different if we viewed learning as a partnership. *"Welcome, we are very happy that you're here. I am Mrs. Prescott, your child's language arts teacher. One of our primary tasks this year is to learn to write properly, and we need your help in teaching your child to write in active voice, as this is something that most don't do well. Since the idea of active and passive voice is confusing to most of us, I am providing some links to a few websites that might be helpful, and we have coordinated with the local library to offer joint parent-student writing workshops every Saturday morning if that is more convenient. Please make yourselves at least somewhat aware of this important skill, so you can help your son or daughter."*

The teacher might go so far as to ask the parents to coauthor their child's papers each week, with a focus on shared learning. *"Please write about a topic of your choice, not mine. Focus on something that your family has an interest in, and please put both of your names on the paper as we are all in this together."*

Yes, of course. This may be a family engagement bridge too far, but the concept of joint learning activities is not unthinkable. In fact, if coauthoring a paper is so far-fetched as to be unworkable, what do we assume is occurring when we ask parents to read to their children? To be fair, let's consider some tough questions.

Is the idea of shared ownership of instruction outside the reach of most parents? *Maybe.* Do parents have the time? *Certainly not.* These are legitimate questions and real obstacles, though not insurmountable. Of course, if writing in active voice is a bit too much for some, then how about teaming with parents or local agencies on the workings of local government or the housing market or environmental issues?

Lest we think that our communities are not equipped to take this on, it is probably important to point out (with no hint of sarcasm) that we are teaching content meant for children. This means that our teachers and leaders must examine their own biases as to how much the public really knows about reading, math, science, and social studies (probably much more than we think) and how willing they are to help tutor their own children and others (probably much more than we think).

For those who suggest that having parents help with academic matters is idealistic or unrealistic, we have to question if what we are describing is more deficit thinking. "My parents can't do that or won't do that" sounds a lot like what we say about children. The critics are probably correct in saying that most parents *can't* or *won't*, though it is not because they can't or won't but because they cannot envision such a relationship, because they are stuck in the current model, and because they have never been asked.

EMPOWERMENT SCHOOLS AND COMMUNITIES

As we ponder what this new system might look like, we can agree that it is going to take a while to get there. The entry points provided above are just beginnings and are not scalable solutions in and of themselves. In applying further pressure, it may be possible to find a common action that schools can give over to families and communities to own and manage. If we accomplish nothing else, these discussions will require school systems to open their doors and share in some of what they do in making schools go. This may lead to even better options. Let's consider some ideas that might be worth discussing:

Student Scheduling

The days have long passed for school counselors to be solely responsible for scheduling students. Though we have a desperate need for counseling in our schools (in fact, we need more of it), there are many important tasks outside of scheduling that demand a counselor's attention, from socioemotional support to college planning.

Much like colleges have done for years, school districts could give course requests and even scheduling over to students and families. In fact, a few schools and districts have already piloted this work. This is not about counselor workload as much as it is about shared ownership of key academic decisions, like what courses to take. The more the system transfers ownership of these decisions to students and parents, the more our families become true partners in the mission of college and career readiness.

Data-Sharing

The idea that schools know more about student performance data and each child's strengths and weakness than parents do seems backward somehow. We can certainly envision a system in which data are constructed to inform students and parents first and foremost so they can adequately chart a path for academic improvement. It is not out of bounds to expect parents to know how many words their children read per minute or how efficient they are with fractions without counting on the teacher to tell them.

Though nearly all school districts provide parent access to grades, test scores, and attendance records, access to information is a far cry from usefulness or empowerment. We are not yet close to authentic, shared ownership of student data. The good news is that powerful strategies on how to match families to student data and learning goals are arriving fast, thanks to researchers like Harvard professor Karen Mapp and others.

It should be noted that some school districts are still moving with some trepidation, as if we have something to hide. Of course, history has taught us that knowledge is power and that power must shift from schools to families. Author and futurist John Naisbitt (1982) puts it this way: "The new source of power is not money in the hands of a few, but information in the hands of many."

Tutoring/Mentoring

We can certainly agree that all children would benefit from an adult mentor, even those who are doing well in school. Surely, this is something that schools should not own and manage alone. Even as many companies step forward to provide tutors and mentors, the apparatus and decisions that make it go are most often managed by local schools (from fingerprinting to scheduling).

This is the opposite of shared ownership. It is the opposite of community empowerment. Without too much difficulty, an advanced system for locating, vetting, training, and assigning mentors could be owned and operated entirely by a municipality, police department, or Chamber of Commerce with little to no involvement by the schools. Yes, we know. They don't have the time to do all of that work. Neither do our schools.

COMMUNITY BABY STEPS

Case in Point: Literacy/Numeracy

It is probably best for communities to start with something that everyone can agree on. We all know that students with deeper and richer reading and math skills find school easier and more rewarding. These antecedent skills lead to all kinds of hidden successes later on that most do not see. Let's skip over the obvious benefit that mastering advanced reading and math skills has in obtaining higher grades and test scores. Instead, let's go straight into how those skills connect to greater confidence, less frustration, and more efficient time management.

While we know that students who master basic math skills typically make better grades in math, it may surprise you to find out that those students also spend less mental energy doing the math problems that are assigned to them. Let's see why that is by asking any of us to solve a typical multiplication problem that a young student might encounter: $20 \times 9 = $ ____.

In arriving at our answers, we are likely to fall into one of two categories. We are either those brilliant persons who knew the answer without even thinking about it or those who stared and stared for several moments before reaching our conclusions (*note: I used a calculator*). Why does this matter?

Because those who immediately knew the answer expended much less mental energy than those who struggle with problems like these before finally figuring them out.

This means that those who master simple tasks without thinking about them (which is called *automaticity*) have plenty of cognitive energy left to take on harder tasks. The same is true for students who have advanced vocabularies in finding their reading assignments easier. This logic plays out over and over again in school and life. The more we know things to automaticity, from the parts of the body to the branches of government, the easier it is for us to handle the harder concepts when presented with them. In outlining a broader community model, we could certainly create vibrant local partnerships specific to teaching our children these foundational skills.

Any collective impact initiative that leads to increased mastery for students of basic reading, math, science, and social studies concepts will free up schools to focus on more complex skills and increase the academic and social confidence of children. This is quite naturally aligned to the skills presented within the Community Wheel and provides endless opportunities for communities to jump in and begin this work right now.

In fact, there is too much at stake to sit on the sidelines. It is not an exaggeration to say that children who do not learn such things by the time they leave elementary school have a stronger likelihood of losing confidence in themselves as learners, and that can manifest itself over time as permanent self-doubt and even self-loathing.

Let us dig a bit deeper in discovering how this happens, beginning with an example using sight words. Sight words are those simple words that comprise most of all written language and that all children must learn early in school so they can recognize and pronounce them at a glance, with no energy expended. For purposes of this example, we will focus on sight words, though mastering other high frequency words is equally critical to reading fluency.

No matter what word lists your school or district prefers, most educators agree that our youngest children must learn these common words (such as *hot* and *cold*) without hesitation very early on to prevent lingering deficiencies that will carry into middle and high school. The same can be said for mastering roots and prefixes. The notion that some of our elementary school children do not acquire such things by the end of each grade is a school problem (yes), a parent problem (yes), and can quickly become a community problem (yes).

This is why skills always precede ability, and ability precedes confidence, a critical progression found among all people. This common learning progression is presented via each of the wheel graphics with the antecedent skills found closer to the center, as they are typically mastered first. A deep understanding of how we learn is quite affirming in knowing, without question, that each child can become a confident learner if we can guarantee that he or she has gained the requisite skills and agency required.

As with other examples provided in this text, the selection of sight words or math facts as community endeavors are only possibilities to consider. Each community's needs are different, and unique solutions must be designed by local stakeholders. Similar community initiatives could be designed around teaching things like civility, pride, creativity, dignity, or others. No matter how they choose to do it, it is possible for communities to stand together and collectively agree that no children will exit school without the skills they need to succeed.

SO WHAT'S THE HOLDUP? SYSTEMS RESISTANCE

At a recent leadership conference, a young principal was relaying an intriguing idea about parent involvement to a colleague from another school district. The new principal was making the case that her parents were key players in reshaping her school, and she was floating an idea about how to harness that potential.

Her suggestion was met with a quizzical look from her colleague and a quick brush-off at the notion that parent engagement was any kind of real solution. Like many such overtures, her idea was chided as a "pie-in-the-sky" concept that is mentioned by those who have no experience in schools and no sense of how little our parents wish to help. *What we need most from our parents is for them to bring their kids to school and stay out of the way.*

This conversation says a great deal about the struggles in our schools and the very real difference between what we say and what we mean. It seems prudent to point out the most obvious failure in logic that this example provides us. Even if we count those students who come to school every day, too many of them underperform and too many do not graduate.

If we are primed to tell our parents that they should "stay away and let us do our jobs," then we should prepare an answer when one of them comes back with: "We've already tried that and it didn't work. We have stayed away. We have dropped our kids off every day for many years and they are still not reading at grade level."

The conversation between the two principals is not meant to shame our leaders or the system. The veteran principal is simply expressing something that we see too often in our industry: systems resistance. Without even realizing it, she is expressing her fears that the system as presently designed may be inadequate. Her conditioned response is to convince herself and others that any innovative idea for improvement is uninformed or undoable. The system is fine. It's the kids or the parents who are the problem.

These sentiments are common among large systems of all sorts. As a reminder, it may be time that we return to the Dream-Reality Paradox presented in chapter 1. Though leaders are quick to speak at a Rotary luncheon about our dreams and plans for change, the reality is that we do not execute those plans with enough fidelity or urgency, in large part because the system does not want to change that much in the first place.

While every school and school district seeks to advance and improve, it is rare to find a system that is willing to take the risks necessary to realize dramatic improvement. The issue of intent is a precarious one in making this claim, for no one is suggesting that our leaders are aware of their resistance or that they are plotting against change. Most leaders want change, but they cannot find success amid so much self-doubt and second-guessing from the system itself. The result? Lots of talk. Little change. Big hat. No cattle.

SOME SERIOUS CONTROL ISSUES: HOMEOSTASIS

The familiar cycle of big ideas and little results is not likely to change as long as our systems and the leaders who manage them have the same endgame: keeping the system stabilized. The system does not seek a better way, because it is not in the DNA of systems to do so. The system will only change when acted upon from the outside, when such changes are required to remain alive. "In rapidly changing and turbulent environments—characteristics of our current era—there is a temptation in the educational community to protect the system against those external forces" (Banathy, 1992, p. 44).

The result is a self-regulating, self-sustaining process called *homeostasis*. The process of change is hindered by the system's attempt to maintain its body temperature. Too hot and we end up with a fever. Too cold and we might freeze to death. The risks are just too great to push too hard. Though social systems like schools are generally regarded as open systems, we tend to close ourselves off because it's safer that way.

Of course, all of this is backward. Organizations are open systems because of their ongoing exchanges of energy, matter, and information with their environments. The back-and-forth relationship between the organization and its environment allows for the system to evolve just enough to remain viable (homeostasis) without pushing on the system too hard (equilibrium). The definition of organizations as social systems can be traced to groundbreaking research from Daniel Katz and Robert Khan from 1960s and 1970s.

New theories presented in those days rejected the traditional notion that organizations were isolated from their communities. In fact, it is now believed that vibrant systems like organizations are in a constant state of inputs and outputs. Success occurs when energy is transformed and something new is produced, a product is exported into the environment, and the system maximizes its ratio of imported to expended energy. The balance of inputs and exports includes things like raw material, social and financial capital, employee satisfaction, and community goodwill.

Even among change agents with sound strategic plans, their inputs and outputs often get out of balance because leaders end up managing the side effects of their efforts, the distractions and resistors, instead of the strategic solutions themselves (Wheatley and Kellner-Rogers, 1998). Complicating matters further for school systems is an endless number of actions, outcomes, and goals. In fact, a key characteristic of an open system is something called *purposiveness*. Some systems have a singular purpose, which is classified as a "unitary" system. Other systems have many purposes, sometimes even conflicting ones. These are called "pluralistic" systems.

Betts warns us that leaders in education are often unaware or unwilling to take inventory of the many competing interests they are managing. "We have attempted to treat education as a unitary system, but in reality it is highly pluralistic with many conflicting goals. The compromises that we have reached by applying old paradigms in a new context are proving to be unsatisfactory, but paradigm paralysis prevents us from seeing what is really needed" (Betts, 1992, p. 40).

A POSSIBLE WAY OUT: EMPOWERING SYSTEMS

The rigid structures and inflexible relationships found within highly complex systems are made worse under the direction of leaders who want solutions of their own making within systems of their own design. The problem with demanding such a high degree of command and control is that our systems must continually interact with the people and communities they serve. As one might expect, most people are not so quick to be shaped by others.

To be perfectly clear, it is hardly reasonable for a leader to design a system without public input and then expect the public to just deal with it. Of course, the solution is to create organizations that "mirror's life's adaptability, diversity, and creativity" (Capra and Luisi, 2014, p. 316). As such, the question we should pose for system leaders is not whether they are leading an open system, but whether the system is open enough.

The future of schools will involve some expansion of system boundaries to include a broader community of stakeholders who engage the system and benefit from it. As we have learned from the travel industry, a school system is not sustainable if it only works for those who are employed by it. All profitable companies win when they invest in structures that work for their customers. As a consumer, the system works for *me*. It is easy for *me* to navigate. It makes *my* life easier. In the end, everyone is satisfied because the system works for all.

The answer for school systems involves a greater degree of shared ownership with our students, parents, and community leaders in figuring this out. If we do this well, the system will maintain sufficient balance. Along the way, the system must decide which entities are allowed in and which are left to observe from the outside. This will be tricky business.

There is no benefit to the system in delaying this work, because the longer we wait, the harder it will get. In the context of the current generation of young people, we may soon find a grassroots effort emerging in which students and parents rise up and take some control of their own. This is not likely to be a radical attempt to defeat the system (though that is possible), but it may be a way that our customers create to work around the system. Young adults are already comfortable with these non-linear solutions as a result of their experience with social networks. *"We don't need you. We recognize that you exist, but we will work around you more than with you."*

One method to manage such a revolution is to organize it. We have already embraced the practice of professional learning communities (PLCs) or networks (PLNs), so inviting community members or parents into existing structures might be the way to go. If students are bent on starting some sort of grassroots campaign, they could be swayed to form a network in partnership with the school system that empowers them instead of limiting their ideas and influence.

Of course, if we allow others to offer their suggestions, someone has to be brave enough to consider them. If we are not too careful, we might actually uncover a novel concept or two. We might even find our game changer. Systems science tells us that connecting parts that are not normally aligned can lead to profound solutions. For lasting change to occur in any system, the concept of *emergence* (or emergent properties) must be in play. These are the novel properties that emerge from the unique relationships of the parts. They are not found anywhere presently in the system. They are truly novel and would not have been discovered without the formation of new relationships (Capra and Luisi, 2014).

We see the concept of emergence in the classical sciences, but also in cybernetics, nonlinear dynamics, and even music theory. This idea is typically born out of disequilibrium. We don't even see it coming. In organizations, it happens when someone mentions something that nobody has considered before. As you might guess, the system will resist the idea at first, because it simply cannot handle the suggestion being made. Still, if this novel idea continues to be bandied about, the system will be forced to change and a new kind of order will be formed that wasn't even considered before. In truth, only a system in search of solutions will ever find them, and only the bravest will cast a lever long enough to move the world.

Chapter Six

A Roadmap for Evolving Systems

The secret recipe for successful ventures is three parts innovation, two parts resourcefulness, and at least one part sheer trust and will. The lessons learned from successful corporate ventures, inspiring civic endeavors, and superstar public schools are the subject of countless books and movies in our never-ending fascination with what works. Though we may debate the attributes of success, most would agree that we know it when we see it.

There is something about hard-won endeavors that is so alluring that we find it difficult to avoid staring at them and wondering how they did it. We don't have to look far in searching out popular examples like Apple Computers or Pixar Animation Studios. The rise of these companies from intriguing concept to tepid interest to universal rejection to dogged determination to faithful execution and unimaginable comeback could be blueprints for those hoping to push their school systems to incredible heights.

In truth, the greatest of great ventures have always found success in transformative places that exist somewhere beyond corporate structures, business plans, and spreadsheets. In one form or another, such ventures operate in ways that those inside *and* those outside the system find purposeful and meaningful. In a highly compelling manner, the system itself is both self-actualized and self-actualizing at the same time. What results is an experience that is both profitable and memorable for everyone involved, including those who encounter the system for the very first time.

Schools should have that type of effect on people, even if no one ever makes a movie about it. To get closer to such a place, schools and local communities must pursue much loftier heights in their expectations for themselves and the children they serve. Which begs this question: Can a school, school district, or even a neighborhood mature and evolve as a child does? In viewing these systems in more human terms, we have to ponder whether such entities can reach levels of awareness that might be described as metacognitive, enlightened, or even moral.

In short, all this talk of self-actualization among our children begs the question about whether any system that is not self-actualized in its own right (or at least not well on its way) can produce outcomes that aspire to such ends. In the case of schools, it is hard to fathom a school and faculty that is not self-actualized producing graduates who are.

A NEW HIERARCHY OF SOCIAL SYSTEMS

School systems are social systems or what some call "human systems." The entire structure is built around people, with planned social interactions and (get this) with a common sense of purpose. School systems, neighborhood associations, and even political parties are social systems that (if fully functioning) are designed to produce a great deal of energy and, hopefully, synergy around a common cause that brings together people and processes in connected and meaningful ways.

As strange as it seems, it is possible to hold these systems accountable for maturing and growing in the same way we hold our young people accountable. The hierarchy provided (figure 6.1) is designed to frame such a conversation. It is offered to anyone within any type of system that is set on a course to transform from barely functioning to highly sophisticated. It provides context in considering the question that was posed previously about whether a system can have high expectations for the people within the system without having high expectations for the system itself.

In the science of systems, the range of growth or evolution is described as moving from "simple to complex" or from "immature to mature." Within this figure, those terms are used in presenting a hierarchy for social systems in relatable ways for leaders of human systems like schools and communities. The figure is designed to describe a system's growth as moving from "highly simple" (functional) to "highly complex" (sophisticated) in two critical components of human systems: *competence* and *connectivity*.

In understanding what is being implied here, let us be clear that no system can be fully mature (self-actualized) until it is fully competent and fully connected. To frame what this means, let's imagine what a school or school district would look like if it was functioning adequately per its day-to-day operations, but was not truly inspiring its employees and students and not producing dramatic results. In fact, it is fair to say that this description probably fits many schools and systems.

To the casual observer, everything appears to be in order. The system has some structure to it. There are plans and processes in place. Some successes are evident. System leaders can point to a top-notch school here or an award-

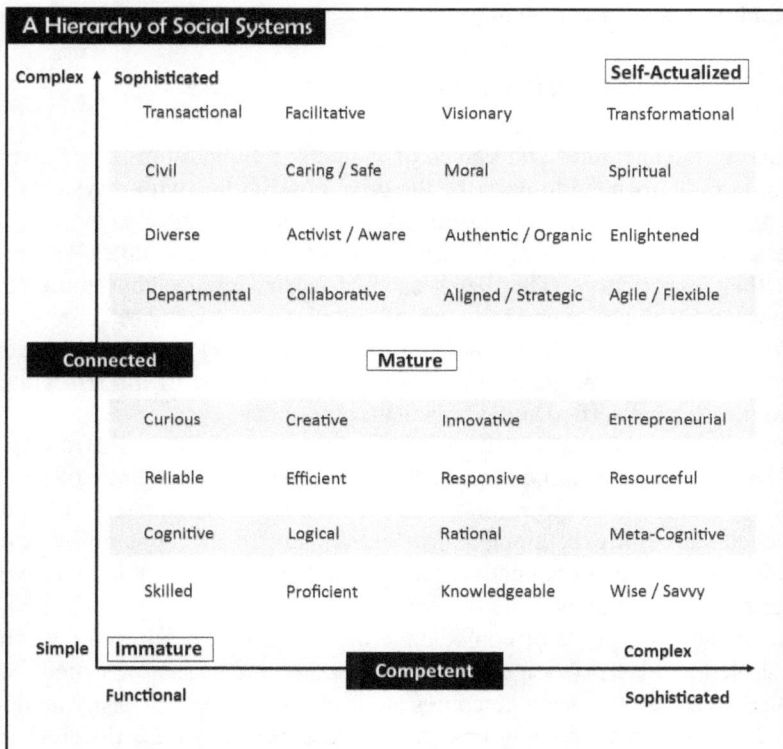

Figure 6.1.   A Hierarchy of Social Systems

winning program there, all the while other schools are not meeting their full potential. Students are only somewhat engaged. Parents are only somewhat interested. The community is only somewhat proud.

Upon close inspection, we may find that a system like this one is not all it can be because the system itself is only functionally skilled and credentialed, only somewhat consistent and reliable, and highly departmentalized (hidden behind walls and cubicles). Yes, the system is self-sufficient and operational, possibly without conflict. Yes, it employs people who generally get along with each other. It provides an adequate service to those who interact with it (e.g., parents). This type of system might be described as civil, transactional, and efficient.

A system like this one is not broken. In fact, it is typical. Still, it has much room to grow and may not even realize its potential. It stands in stark contrast to a system that is highly functional, highly sophisticated, and highly mature. The system does not yet realize the success it could have if it just sprinkled in a bit more innovation, resourcefulness, trust, and will. Let's ponder for a moment what such a system might look like.

HIGHLY COMPETENT SYSTEMS

Presenting the attributes and values of systems in human terms like *competent* or *wise* is intended to describe the great possibilities within systems that dare to know more and be more. These terms also serve to deepen our understanding of systems as alive, with the ability to learn, falter, and grow from their experiences. This helps each of us to view systems thinking in more relatable ways, even if the use of superlatives like "wise" creates discomfort for those who shy away from the hard-to-swallow notion that some systems are not as enlightened as others. In the context of modern culture, social norms have shifted and words matter more than ever.

For purposes of this text, it may help the reader to know that the terms used are not absolutes and are used only to distinguish degrees of growth within systems. To be clear, the terms used are not to be equated with cultural debates around exceptionalism or extremism. In fact, this entire text is designed to elevate our collective dialogue and avoid the unproductive wrangling around such things.

Moreover, the range of competence described in the figure above from low-skilled to wise-savvy is not exclusive to any one learner or system, with the added caution that such outcomes are aspirational and not easily attained. Describing a system as being wise or resourceful is not much different than describing those qualities within each of us. As individuals, what would our day-to-day work and interactions look like if we wanted others to regard us as wise or resourceful or flexible or entrepreneurial?

Whatever responses come to mind, we have to question whether the same qualities can be required of the system itself. In the case of a highly competent school or district, such a system would provide school and field experiences with such high degrees of purpose and ingenuity that each and every student would leave us with a deep understanding and appreciation of many, many cultures, disciplines, and real-world concerns.

Actually, the system itself would be in such a constant state of learning that it would function in a manner not unlike what was asked of our leaders: facilitating instructional change, fostering meaningful relationships, navigating community connections, and seeing around the bend. The system would be profoundly self-aware as to anticipate the changing dynamics of learners months and years in advance. These are things that a minimally functioning system would not recognize or even think possible.

To further our thinking, we will connect the growth of a system (a single department, a central office, a local government) to the plight of a new teacher. While there are a few exceptions here and there, it is widely accepted that new teachers encounter similar challenges and growing pains no matter the school or school district. To be sure, it is incredibly difficult to be a new teacher.

No matter where we work, we can likely agree that our expectations for new teachers are modest. We hope that they survive the first few months, grow in their skill sets along the way, and build positive relationships with their students and colleagues. Oh, and we pray that they don't quit halfway through the year.

Drawing on our long history of hiring and observing new teachers, we can say that most enter the profession with the basic skills needed to do their jobs, with some mastery of the requisite content (though probably no more than that), and with some degree of kindness and caring for children. If this is true, then we also know that arriving to the profession with these foundational skills is a far cry from being wise or enlightened.

Our new teachers are simply not there. They are not likely to be visionaries in their profession. They are not likely to be highly creative yet in their planning and agile in their decision-making. Certainly, they are not yet savvy in their handling of students, parents, and administrators. They don't need to apologize, for they are not broken. They are just new.

Let us contrast our visual of a fledging teacher with the skills and talents of the strongest, most experienced teachers in the field. In nearly every case, the differences are so stark that they defy description. In fact, the advanced skill sets of our best teachers are so artful and nuanced that we struggle to define them adequately in the research.

To the bewilderment of the new teacher, the master teacher has reached such a level of competence and dexterity that the new teacher is left wide-eyed and confused. The new teacher is so far from that reality that he or she cannot imagine aspiring to such heights. In truth, he or she might be just trying to survive the day. Let us consider then what the reaction might be if we suggested to this teacher that he or she was operating in ways that were unwise or unenlightened. Yes, that would be hard to hear, though not fully inaccurate.

The same can be said for school systems themselves. In similar ways, this is why it is so hard to have substantive discussions about growing our systems. No one wants to admit that we are not yet wise or enlightened, that we are so far removed from being a master teacher that we cannot even consider the possibilities. Like the new teacher, we don't have to apologize for the growth we have before us. We just have to want it.

This can be quite difficult for leaders who have a hard time admitting that they don't have it all figured out. Still, we must get there, to a safe place where honesty and authenticity breeds integrity and innovation. If we do not, we may find that our current system is extolling the excellence and artfulness of its current practices while sounding somewhat like the new teacher who doesn't yet know what he doesn't know.

In supporting the growth of highly competent school systems, the following five entry points are provided to school leaders who are engaging in this work:

1. Hire and retain highly competent and highly effective employees.
2. Establish structures that empower highly effective employees to flourish and lead.
3. Develop a work culture that is open to new ideas and rewards enterprise/experimentation.
4. Develop a work culture in which knowledge, information, and ideas are shared and not held.
5. Adopt employee appraisal models that are highly reflective, self-affirming, and self-motivating.

HIGHLY CONNECTED SYSTEMS

In returning to our example of a school or district that is functioning at a minimal level, there is more missing than system expertise or savvy. A strong thread of connectivity among people and processes is also hard to find. A system that is functioning at less-than-optimal levels tends to either breed isolation or not recognize it. These systems are largely top-down in their structures and highly departmentalized (even siloed). In fact, these systems are sometimes so fractured in their mission and purpose that the people who work there are pursuing dissimilar or even counter aims.

Trouble signs emerge when employees or departments don't share the same vision or don't understand each other's role in executing the vision. There is little coherence in thought or actions among leaders and employees. As a result, the focus is less on system outcomes and more on individual or departmental successes. When this happens in school districts, there is likely to be a quiet sense of frustration across the landscape in blaming the students for not working hard enough, their parents for not caring enough, or teachers and leaders for not doing enough.

Let's return again to the struggles that our new teachers face in understanding how this plays out. There is a good chance that a new teacher is not connected to many others at the school. He or she may be working (and venting) in isolation and may see no true relevance to the curriculum that he or she has been asked to teach. In a very short time, a once optimistic new teacher becomes increasingly distrustful of the system and blames the district, the principal, the parents, or the students for the mess we are in.

Just down the hallway, a master teacher works in constant interaction with her students and colleagues. She invents new curricula, experiments with new assessments, and turns her lessons over to kids. She sees alignment and meaning in her work by connecting the lessons to students' lives and to the betterment of the communities they live in. All the while, she engages with her fellow teachers through common planning and social media conversations. She is not frustrated. She is invigorated.

In the same manner that successful teachers thrive, systems can as well. As human systems, schools and school districts have unique opportunities to build deep personal and professional connections among departments, employees, families, and children. In fact, a system cannot adequately describe itself as highly mature without these purposeful connections in place. This goes much further than a simple alignment of goals and outcomes. This has much more to do with planned interactions that inspire and engage teachers and students, and not simply for the sake of inspiration but for the sake of achievement.

Within highly connected systems, schools prioritize collaboration among teachers, leaders, and students. Such systems value teacher and student agency, voice, and choice as key ingredients to deeper learning. We see greater student and district involvement in civic initiatives like local elections, veteran's organizations, parks and recreation, and cultural celebrations.

In pursuit of greater connectivity, such systems would seek out diverse opinions and increase opportunities for honest dialogue and out-of-the-box suggestions. Outcome metrics such as employee satisfaction, teacher retention, school climate, and community confidence would be valued as much as reading scores and graduation rates. Information-sharing and decision-making would be highly transparent. Each of these changes would lessen the power structures found within most hierarchical models in favor of distributed leadership, collective struggle, and combined impact.

In supporting the growth of highly connected school systems, the following five entry points are provided to school leaders who are engaging in this work:

1. Hire and retain a diverse workforce (gender, race, background, attitudes, and beliefs).
2. Establish structures that connect people to people in professional and personal ways.
3. Establish structures that encourage discussion within safe and supportive workplaces.
4. Hire and promote leaders who are highly relational and servant-minded. Distribute leadership.
5. Communicate with and involve those outside the system in genuine and purposeful ways.

In returning to Pixar studios as an example, there is something else worth noting in understanding the conditions for its success. In the company's earliest days, despite financial struggles and industry critics, something important was happening deep within the workings of the studio that was not yet noticeable to those on the outside. The small team of animators who imagined new methods for creating successful feature films also crafted a work culture and corporate structures required to meet their ambitious outcomes. This began with hiring highly competent employees to work in cross-disciplinary teams and within cross-functional departments.

More intriguing than that, company leaders did not favor these structures simply for the purpose of designing a creative workplace. In fact, many companies already tried that and failed. At Pixar, they imagined a work culture built around high degrees of competency and strong connectivity that was in direct alignment with their vision for creating high-impact products (feature films in this example). More to the point, the system was designed to ensure that those outside the company (audiences and fans) would experience deep personal connections to the company itself (to Pixar) through the human emotions expressed in its films.

This was not simply a company out to make movies. This was a company with a soul.

If school systems are to reach such heights, vibrant new organizations must be built that emphasize greater connectivity and deeper purpose. Even organizations can accomplish such things. In his revolutionary (and radical) text *The Living Company*, Arie de Geus (1997) poses a question with far-reaching implications for school districts: what if we thought of a company as a living being?

In asking this question, de Geus challenges the orthodox view of corporations as machines, as nonhuman entities conceived many years ago by their builders, controlled by their current operators, and occasionally retooled by management. The company is the central entity. Those who work for it are simply resources to be managed. Those who interact with it are merely inputs to be processed (de Geus, 1997).

In stark contrast, the idea of viewing a company as a living organism provides for natural growth and maturity for the company itself and characterizations of its success in more human terms. The company has an identity. It has purpose and beliefs unto itself that are expressed through its actions. If this is true, then the company has the ability to care for (or not) those who interact with it. It has the ability to value (or not) those who are impacted by its decisions.

Make no mistake: the company is still designed for profit and success. It is still designed to win. The system is not created to care for and value others for altruistic reasons alone. It is designed as a system of high character so as to impact corporate success, industry achievement, and even the bottom line.

As you might expect, this is incredibly difficult for current managers to conceive of since most grew up in an age of assembly lines and top-down corporate hierarchies. In the same way, leaders within school districts struggle to imagine solutions outside the current accountability measures, employee appraisal frameworks, and school bell schedules. We are so deeply conditioned and bound by such things that our minds cannot easily unravel them.

THE HISTORY OF THE FUTURE: WHAT WOULD MASLOW DO?

In stretching our imaginations, it is only logical that we return to Maslow to render his thoughts on the matter. It may be surprising for some to find out that Maslow wrote extensively on management and work culture throughout his storied career. His collection of journal entries on leadership was released under the title *Maslow on Management* (Maslow, Stephens, and Heil, 1998). It has been reprinted and cited countless times.

Maslow was not afraid to explore some Utopian thinking that strayed a bit from hard science, even from the softer side of human science. He fashioned what he called normative or ideal social psychology. In essence, he subscribed to the science of possibilities. As Maslow himself described it, he sought to uncover "the culture that would be generated by one thousand self-actualizing people on some sheltered island where they would not be interfered with" (Maslow, 1959).

In keeping with his fascination for such things, he observed successful people and wrote down what he saw. He was interested in true leadership, in the actual game changers. If he were here, he would tell us that he wasn't much for those who only talked a good game. "That's the way you tell the difference between fruitfulness and sterility, between talkers and doers, between people who change the world and people who are helpless in it" (Maslow, Stephens, and Heil, 1998).

Maslow had no problem with those who were not equipped to lead as long as they were not leading. He suggested that they join the League of Responsible Citizens, there among the "freeloaders, hangers-on, mere talkers, the permanent passive students who study forever with no results" (Maslow, Stephens, and Heil, 1998, p. 5).

Maslow described his philosophy as "enlightened management." He preferred leaders who were highly competent and creative and who empowered their employees. He observed success in companies that valued employee growth and competence and were intentional in creating synergy among them. Maslow frames it this way: "That which is beneficial to the individual is beneficial to all. High synergy cultures are secure, benevolent, and high in morale. Low synergy cultures are insecure, in conflict, and low in morale" (Maslow, Stephens, and Heil, 1998, p. 24).

Maslow's use of the word *synergy* is important in connecting his findings to what we have learned from systems theory. One surefire way to generate synergy in authentic ways is in developing deep relationships among the parts. What results is a more unified whole. "If the old paradigms won't work, something fundamentally better suited to the task is needed, a paradigm that illuminates the whole, not just the parts; one that is synthetic, rather than analytic; one that integrates, rather than differentiates" (Betts, 1992, p. 38).

Betts uses the metaphor of heat in a thermodynamic system to show us that a relationship among the elements is maintained by an exchange of energy and by a difference in energy potential among the elements, which allows for a healthy interchange. This kind of energy manifests itself within school systems when we create opportunities for interaction, where employees and students and community members share ideas and partner in solutions. These interactions generate an exchange of energy and, ultimately, synergy.

On the contrary, Betts (1992) tells us that a closed system cannot import energy and, as such, cannot generate a sufficient amount of energy internally to replace what is lost. Ultimately, this leads to entropy and system failure.

SEASONED LEADERSHIP: PROCEEDING WITH CAUTION

The work of systems design (and redesign) is not for the faint of heart. In fact, leaders who do not execute this work from the core principles outlined in this text can fail miserably. This is called systemic failure. It occurs when the system does not probably support and align the subsystems that need to work well together for success to occur.

In William Tate's book *The Search for Leadership: An Organizational Perspective* (2009), he lists the following factors that can lead to widespread failure: confused goals, weak system-wide understanding, flawed design, inadequate feedback, poor cooperation, and lack of accountability.

Leaders can combat these factors by building organizations around collaborative goal-setting, meaningful employee development, authentic communication, incentives and rewards, and mutual accountability. The endgame is the success of each individual and, in turn, dramatic results for the system as a whole (along with fewer random victories). "The aim is to focus on what binds individuals together and what binds systems together rather than functional silo performance" (Tate, 2009).

As leaders venture into the deep waters of systems change, they should be wary of the hazards beneath the surface. Among the most telling cautions offered by researchers is that any conclusions leaders reach about the current structures and needs for the system must be carefully triangulated so fatal mistakes are not made. Keen observation is critical in remaining aware of false assumptions and misinformation. Meadows (2008) warns that if we are serious about viewing a system as a living being then we must know well its personality: "Before you disturb the system in any way, watch how it behaves.... Watch it work. Learn its history" (p. 170).

Assumptions must be balanced against hard data because observations of living systems do not always match the data measured by their outcomes. In school districts, a great number of mistaken assumptions about academic improvement, culture, and climate can be made if accountability metrics are not weighed against observational and perception data.

Without shrewd inquiry, leaders cannot assume that improved attendance means that students are finding school more enjoyable. They cannot conclude that an increase in employee retention rates is evidence of employee satisfaction. They cannot surmise that parents really like their schools just because they are not complaining to the front office.

Only the deftest leaders are aware of how the system is intended to work versus how it actually works. Those leaders do not assume that the system is operating as designed on paper. They are a lot more perceptive than that. "Watching what really happens, instead of listening to people's theories of what happens, can explode many careless causal hypotheses" (Meadows, 2008, p. 171).

Systems as they exist on paper or in PowerPoint presentations are rational, but those same systems are under constant attack from irrational forces that have their own interests at stake. If left unchecked, they can form systems of their own called "shadow systems." According to Tate (2009), this is where things like power, greed, and politics reside: "The (shadow) system can confuse, overpower, block, and fail leadership." This is a key reason why whole system failure can coexist alongside the successes of key parts, and why leaders must be attuned to what we have learned about systems as everchanging and ever-nuanced.

A SHADOW SOLUTION: DECENTRALIZING THE SYSTEM

While the point was made in the previous chapter that upending the entire system (full-on revolution) is risky at best, some immediate pressures could be brought to bear to move things along a bit faster (forced evolution). One such idea is to introduce parallel systems that are at work to propel innovation and improvement for the good of the entire system and not to please selfish interests. We will call these shadow solutions.

These solutions will demand greater maturity from the system itself. They will certainly require that the system give greater voice over to schools, teachers, and students, even to the point of (yes) shared decision-making and (yes) shared power. This is a step in decentralizing the system in a manner (if done slowly) that is still comfortable for the system itself. In fact, this could be accomplished in highly creative ways (e.g., social media networks, coffee shop PLCs) that are bent on increasing system competence and connectivity.

Steps to increase system maturity can take many forms. Any attempt to reduce bureaucracy, open lines of communication, and increase shared decision-making will go a long way toward self-actualization. As human systems, these steps are especially critical within school districts. It only makes sense that teachers and students feel most comfortable and alive when they search out deeper human understanding through things like communication, co-planning, and co-creating. In putting a finer point on it, a system cannot expect to be highly competent and highly connected within ancient bureaucracies established in the name of hierarchy and stratification.

It's counterintuitive.

This is why it is fair to ask about the system's interest in changing versus holding steady. Do we really want the opinions of others? Do we trust that others might see solutions that we do not? History has taught us that bureaucracies are not very good at empowering people and communities to think for themselves, to imagine, and to lead. This is certainly fixable, especially in school districts that consider it their business to encourage such things. This is where core beliefs matter. This is where mindset means something.

The system simply cannot become self-actualized if its actions don't match its words. The system cannot set goals to get all students to graduate or read at grade level and yet have conditions that would make that unlikely. The system cannot establish a vision around improved collegiality and then create structures that are more isolating than they are collaborative. The words we use and actions we take as leaders contribute to these beliefs.

This is not unlike what we find in classrooms. If a student is valued and supported along the way, he or she can grow in confidence and feel more empowered that "I/we can accomplish anything." By the way, the opposite of this is not pessimism or discouragement but something even worse. It is called "learned helplessness," the damning realization that "I cannot do this. I am not smart. I cannot learn. In fact, I am not even going to try." If we are not careful, employees can fall into similar patterns.

To understand how this plays out across a system of adults and children, we may find that connections and relationships are lacking. We may find a lack of understanding and trust, not so much in leadership, but in the system. If we were honest about our struggles, we would admit that this is a challenge that we must face. Leaders should know that a highly evolved system cannot emerge from such a place.

This work around connections and relationships will require us to involve and empower others in ways that will feel uncomfortable at first. It will require the system itself and the leaders who design it to assume goodwill (not mistrust), wisdom (not ignorance), and goodness (not evil). As leaders of human systems, we must endeavor to understand the people we work with so we can arrive at outcomes that we commonly share. "It seems very clear to me that in an enterprise, if everybody concerned is absolutely clear about the goals and directives and far purposes of the organization, practically all other questions then become simple technical questions of fitting means to the ends" (Maslow, Stephens, and Heil, 1998).

When each of us views the system as having a purpose, we are much more likely to dedicate ourselves to its cause. In connecting systems theory to best practice in education, Banathy calls on leaders to "dedicate ourselves to purpose seeking as a mode of thinking and action" (Banathy, 1992, p. 5).

The truth be told, our students and teachers are seeking greater purpose in the things we have asked them to do, and between the things they see within our schools and those they witness on the outside. Only a self-actualized system can provide them with those answers. Banathy (1992) puts it this way: "There is now a search for establishing a grand alliance of science, philosophy, art, and religion" (p. 6).

And so, let the search for those connections begin. And let our schools lead the way.

Chapter Seven

It's the Ecology, Stupid

The intrinsic sense that all people are connected to each other and to some grand opera is what we are calling "spiritual" for purposes of this text. Across all generations and within all cultures there has been a common quest to uncover that mysterious thing within ourselves that is hard to define and yet defines us nonetheless. This thing evolves within us over time and speaks to us through an inner voice that shapes our core beliefs and our actions.

We cannot deny it, even if we are not sure from where it derives. Many posit that we arrived here from a common being or a common beginning of some sort. Whatever the answer, we must know that each of us exists as part of a broad ecology that forms our mutually assured existence. Whatever we call this connection between things, between *every single thing*, it has not yet been adequately explained by scientists. It is an equation yet unsolved.

This search for answers to life's big questions begins at an early age, even if we don't know it at the time. Schools play a critical role in that development, for these are the places where we learn to think, to question, to appreciate, and to aspire. This entire book is dedicated to that cause. It is a call to action. It seeks to frame some draft thoughts about how we might get there, even if some of the answers are still not known. In fact, this book is not intended to provide the answers as much as it is to ask the questions.

We know this much. If human beings are part of some quest for deeper meaning and connection, then schools must be leading that search on behalf of the searchers, the children seated before us. We owe the kids that much. If we are true to this calling, we can build a consensus of solutions that binds people in a common cause that leads to even greater schools. If we don't, we will continue to devolve into a bureaucracy of teachers and administrators who have no greater purpose than to remain employed, pay our bills, and stay just enough under the radar to survive our thirty years and maybe celebrate a promotion or two along the way.

Yes, of course, all this talk of purpose in our lives and work is spiritual, or "mystical" if that term is a better fit for you. This can all be described as leading from the soul, from a deeply personal place that none of us can articulate nor defend, since we cannot define it anyway. This is where faith and science swoop in to help.

As was presented in chapter 1, scientists, philosophers, and theorists across many disciplines now tell us that everything, in some way, is connected to everything else. They have explored answers in the name of science that provide us some fascinating insights into matters of faith, a glimpse into the complex nature of things unseen.

In returning to the questions posed at the start of this text, these intellectuals are asking things that we must ask as leaders in education and across all organizations. What is the impact of a particular action versus another? What is the true nature of change? To better understand how we got here, let's connect a few dots by providing a historical perspective.

HISTORY AS A GUIDE: A PETRI DISH SOLUTION

As most of us are aware, the critical debates we are having about what is nature and what is truth are not new. In fact, the emergence of science as a wise man's antidote to religious constructions of truth arrived centuries ago with new discoveries in mathematics and astronomy under names like Galileo, Descartes, and Newton.

In pursuit of pure science, Galileo Galilei restricted his studies to that which could be measured and quantified. Not to be outdone, Rene Descartes insisted on dividing complex phenomena into pieces to understand the behavior of the whole by studying the properties of its parts, something we know of as Cartesian Mechanics. A world comprised of living and spiritual beings was now viewed as a machine, which became the dominant metaphor of the modern era (Capra, 1996).

This line of thinking can be traced to Greek atomists, who drew a clear line between spirit and matter. They saw matter as simply dead particles moving in the void. In fact, atoms and void were the only things that really existed. The human description of things, even emotions, was mere perception and not reality. It was atomists who propelled us on a course toward dualism, the separation of body and soul.

Questions like these occupied Western thought for more than two thousand years after the culmination of Greek science and culture in the fifth and fourth centuries BC. It was Aristotle who took on the ambitious idea of codifying scientific thinking, and he believed the most important questions concerned the soul and the divine handiwork he saw as he studied the world around him. The Aristotelian view of things remained unchallenged through the Middle Ages, in part because church leaders supported this line of scholarship.

The Renaissance brought a greater focus on nature and far less tribute was paid to Aristotle and his spiritual leanings. Thanks to an emerging interest in mathematics, scientific theory was celebrated based on experimentation and numbers. This is where Galileo begins his ascension to the priesthood of science (pun intended). The birth of modern science provided a ripe environment for a clear (even extreme) separation of spirit and matter.

Of course, this paved the path in the seventeenth century for Descartes, whose philosophies separated nature into the things of the mind (*res cogitans*) and the things of matter (*res extensa*). Isaac Newton held to this mechanistic world view, and the Newtonian model of the universe dominated all scientific thought for more than two hundred years.

In this world view, everything is strictly observed through a scientific lens, as a grand petri dish that can be placed under a microscope to find the most miniscule solutions to our problems (sometimes called *reductionism*). Every dilemma we face can be dissected and fixed if only we had the time (and a big enough petri dish). Scientists of this sort posit that spiritual things, such as art and beauty, are simply human constructs placed on the tiny strokes of a brush or pen and told through religious texts and lofty verse. These scientists told us then, and some tell us today, that there is nothing we cannot explain, only things that are not fully explored.

LIVING SYSTEMS: ONE GREAT HARMONIOUS WHOLE

Of course, there has been great opposition to this hard-scientific, black-and-white line of thinking, even among the scientific community itself. As we have discussed, many scientists now subscribe to a more global, systems view of the world. They argue that the world and most things in it can come into spectacular view if we pull back the microscope a bit and gaze upon things from a more global view (sometimes called *holism*).

This is the difference in perspectives, one might say, that Google Earth provides us and that we cannot see when we are down on the ground and counting the number of rows left until we are finished cutting the lawn. In fact, we might surmise that there is nothing to behold at all in getting that close. We might decide that it is impossible to appreciate the vast wonder and beauty of Earth if we are too busy tugging at the weeds in the garden. This is probably a good time to remind us what Confucius said: "Everything has beauty, but not everyone sees it."

As you might expect, poets and artists throughout history have offered nearly universal opposition to any hard scientific dissection of the world, tinkering with the parts in search of something they will not find. German writer and philosopher Johann Wolfgang von Goethe joined the Romantic artists and philosophers of the late eighteenth and nineteenth centuries in critiquing the mechanistic worldview put forth by Descartes. Helped along by Einstein's theory of relativity, Goethe explored the beauty and complexity of what he regarded as the "one great harmonious whole."

> You must, when contemplating nature,
> Attend to this, in each and every feature:
> There's nought outside and nought within,
> For she is inside out and outside in.
> Thus will you grasp, with no delay,
> The holy secret, clear as day.
>
> Joy in true semblance take, in any
> Earnest play:
> No living thing is One, I say,
> But always Many.—Goethe, "Epirrhema" (c. 1819)

Influenced by Romantics like Goethe, systems thinking and its primary characteristics emerged simultaneously across several disciplines during the first half of the twentieth century (led in large part by biologists, as previously discussed). Of course, Aristotle, himself a biologist, believed that matter could not exist separately from form, and form had no separate existence from matter.

The concept that we know as systems theory was formalized by an Austrian biologist, Ludwig Von Bertalanffy, as General Systems Theory in the 1930s. Foundational to his theory were the interrelationships between elements in forming the whole. He was certain that a reductionist paradigm only worked for simple problems but did not work for more complex undertakings (say, when several variables are involved).

This kind of thinking brings us back to the hard sciences like physics, because physicists are very much interested in complex undertakings. They have found that the science of living systems (ecologies) cannot be fully realized without a faithful understanding that all of nature is interconnected and belongs to a larger universe. In the end, this is what Capra calls the "very essence of spirituality" (Capra, 2000 [1975], p. 7).

In considering the wide landscape of physicists and philosophers who have commented on such things, it is important that we contemplate the great revelation being suggested by these intellectuals. Even if we fully intend to study the parts of something to understand the whole, what we are likely to find is that there are even more parts to study in an endless search for what the parts are telling us. Like a jigsaw puzzle, we may find that all these pieces we are studying have no purpose at all except to provide us with a view of the whole thing.

We might also find that the puzzle has infinite pieces, and we will never find them all. In the end, we may find that the picture on the box is all that there is, that the whole itself *determines* the behavior of the parts and not the other way around. This is best described by philosopher Christian von Ehrenfels, who suggested that the whole is not just *greater* than but also *other than* the sum of its parts.

If this is so, then we have to view the outcomes that we all seek, the alluring and inspiring visions we have for our organizations, as the only things that matter in the end. In other words, the world is connected, so we might as well get on with it. There is just the whole, just the outcomes, just the realities, just the soul. "The properties of the parts are not intrinsic properties but can be understood only within the context of the larger whole. . . . Ultimately—as quantum physics showed so dramatically—there are no parts at all. What we call a part is merely a pattern in an inseparable web of relationships" (Capra, 1996, pp. 36–37).

STAYING ALIVE: IN SEARCH OF WONDER

The deep connection between mind and spirit is not a new concept if we dare to review what we have learned from ancient cultures across philosophical and spiritual traditions. In fact, for early philosophers (long before we were caught up in separating science from religion), there was no distinction between body and mind and between body and soul.

Across Eastern and Western cultures, we find words for *breath* like *anima* and *spiritus* in Latin, *psyche* and *pneuma* in Greek, and *ruach* in Hebrew. In their own ways, these are ancient conceptions of the soul. They express a sort of insight or intuition that is somehow breathed into each of us. This results in a high degree metacognition—self-awareness—that is unique to human beings and always has been. Capra (2000 [1975]) describes it this way:

> When the new systems science sees mind, or cognition, as the process of life, and an ancient tradition sees spirit as the breath of life, they are really expressing the same insight—one in the technical language of science, the other in the poetic, metaphorical language of spirituality. Spirit is the breath of life. Our spiritual moments are the moments when we feel most alive. In those moments we are also totally aware of our environment. We feel alive with a profound sense of belonging to the whole. (p. 8)

This sense of feeling "most alive" and "totally aware of our environment" is frequently missing among our solutions in education and among related social sciences. That is why this text has used terms like *systems* and *ecology* to describe a greater purpose and deeper connectivity among the work we do. These terms are designed to challenge our solution sets that are typically applied in fixing one crisis, one department, or one school at a time when we know that will never work.

In fairness to our critics, our schools have come a long way from the cold and dreary places we knew of during the early days of the industrial age. Yes, we are no longer a Dickens novel. In many, many schools, promising experiments in student ownership and engagement are underway, even down to more comfortable furniture in our classrooms. Still, we might wonder what our students would say if we asked them about the last time they felt "most alive" or "totally aware." They are likely to describe all kinds of things, even if none of them are those they have experienced in school.

Throughout this text, we have explored ways that schools and school districts can create this sense of wonder that we all share and that our children desire. In schools, this manifests itself in the material we teach, the ways we teach it, and the connections we form. If done well, we can create school experiences that are transcendent, not just transactional.

What may be lost on some is that these same desires are found among adults. This common sense of wonder and our common pursuit to understand it are things that make us living beings. In fact, they are lacking in many institutions throughout the world today, not just in schools. In large part, this is what is missing across the landscape of our political and social institutions. Politics that unite. Solutions that inspire.

When we complain about local or national politics, we are expressing the same frustrations that our kids do about school. *You mean, this is all there is? Can't we all just get along?* To be fair, these are not new problems, just evolving ones. In many places, our political divisions have become more extreme and our social posture more defensive. Though this book is not constructed to fix our political or social ills, the solutions offered can be viewed as modern approaches to problem-solving for whatever comes our way in the new generation.

As some will remember, one of the defining moments in the presidential election of 1992 was a decision made by the Clinton campaign to focus its message on the economy, in light of country's emerging recession. In narrowing the campaign's themes to a few winning issues, strategist James Carville famously told campaign workers: "It's the economy, stupid." The campaign used the slogan to stay focused on the most serious problems that voters were facing at the time and to avoid being distracted by the little stuff.

Across schools, communities, and even families, people are seeking what they have always been seeking. They seek deep understanding. They wish for something to believe in. They want to know their neighbors better. We all crave civility and dignity, even patriotism. While it may appear that we are caught up in our own lives, in our social media feeds, in our personal brands, and in our political stances, the truth is that we all seek to pull back from the parts that distract us so we can rediscover the whole. For we are no longer interested in the distractions caused by the little stuff.

In fact, the next political or social revolution may not be one that divides us further. It may be one that unites us. Why? Because we have gotten our messaging wrong for far too long, because people want to focus on more serious matters. In fact, we ourselves want to matter. The things we are searching for are connections found within the ecology of people. Turns out, it is no longer the economy. It's the ecology, stupid.

DEEP ECOLOGY DEFINED

All this talk about ecology and systems is highly relevant to our work as leaders as we process what it means for everything to be connected, in both our schools and the communities around us. As we wrestle with this intellectually and reach reasonable conclusions, we cannot help but move out of the world of hard science and into the world of philosophy, from what we know of as "ecology" into what some describe as "deep ecology."

While *ecology* is a scientific term that describes how organisms connect to their environments, *deep ecology* is a philosophical idea that refuses to separate any one thing from anything else nor give any one thing (even human beings) more value than anything else. As a result, deep ecology fuses the material and spiritual worlds—those two realities—into one indistinguishable whole.

Though many branches exist, we will reference deep ecology only from a metaphysical view. We will do so in making the case that there are no discrete entities but only one unbroken whole. As mentioned previously, we can trace the concept of "holism" to Aristotle via his *Metaphysics*. In a modern context, the philosophy of deep ecology is attributed to Norwegian philosopher Arne Naess, who coined the phrase in 1973. Naess approached the concept from a more radical place than we will in connecting the work to social systems, though some of these ideas provide key foundations in forming our assumptions as leaders.

In short, Naess rejected the notion that the higher consciousness of human beings, or even the sensibilities that animals possess, has any more value in the hierarchy of all things than a tree or a blade of grass. If we ride this notion to the end, deep ecology combines both ecological and environmental philosophies that refuse to rank things in relationship to their impact on human beings. Why? Because the delicate balance among all things is only possible due to the complex interrelationships of all organisms within the ecosystem (with no rank order provided).

From a purely environmental standpoint, deep ecologists stand against any destruction of the natural world, as this is perceived as upsetting to the natural order of things. This is closely akin to what we know of Native American and Eastern mysticism that refuses to separate nature from God. From a religious standpoint, this is where things stray from the Western teachings of Christianity and Judaism. As monotheistic religions, each one views God as the creator of all things and mankind as the protector of God's creation. Still, these religions would reject any suggestion that human beings do not exist above other things, as people are said to be created by God in his own image.

Keeping to our promise to avoid religious debate, we will not subscribe to the more controversial positions associated with things like deep ecology. Instead, such philosophies are presented only as a way of viewing the world and our actions within it as equally important and mutually beneficial. In fact, there is simply no rational way to view any one person, policy, solution, or outcome as disconnected from the other or as more substantial than the next. Things are too interrelated for that to be possible.

In understanding the consequence of such things, leaders must be cautious in viewing *smaller* decisions without considering possible effects on the *larger* system. In fact, we see examples time and time again of seemingly inconsequential decisions that upend the delicate balance of the environments we live in and cause lasting and irreversible harm. In making matters more complex, leaders must be considerate of the weighty ethical considerations at stake in valuing all parts of the system as equally important. Why? Because the survival of any one part is dependent on the well-being of the whole.

System thinkers tend to view the terms *holistic* and *ecological* as slightly different in their meanings, and most prefer the term *ecology* when referencing living systems. Capra (1996) warns us that though the term *deep ecology* is a good fit in describing the match between spirituality and reality, it does not begin to describe the variety of related phenomena that are at play in any organization. This includes things such as patriarchy, imperialism, and racism, which are examples of social domination and which are not ecological.

IN SEARCH OF A WORLD SOUL: WHAT WOULD PLATO DO?

In bridging the waters between the way things could be and the way things really are, a new social ecology is emerging that is considerate of the sometimes-destructive nature of people within a world that is constantly searching for something it cannot find. In a uniquely human way, we seek social connections more than ever, even to the point of interacting with people we do not know through social media platforms we do not value.

In truth, we share this common bond because we are all spiritual beings. We are all searching for the same connections, whatever our love language may be. Appreciation. Approval. Admiration. For purposes of this text, we are calling this thing that we all share a soul. In fact, we all have one, even if we don't want to call it that.

Early Greek philosophers did not struggle with such things, in large part because they were not clouded by our modern insistence that we separate science from spiritual matters. They did not (or could not) separate the soul from the mind. The soul was thought to be the connector between what we perceive and what we know, inseparable from the universe. Things did exist, whatever those things were, though none of them had meaning without the perspective that the soul provided. The soul was our source for making sense of things. In fact, it still is.

Of course, this is a point of great debate. We all know that the science of the physical world has collided many times with the philosophies of the metaphysical, a clash of ideas that began at least 2,500 years ago. Even after endless experimentation and mathematical formalism (or maybe *because* of these things), Western thinkers have come back around again to embracing the spirituality of things.

> When spirituality is understood as inner growth, associated with the experience of a profound sense of connectedness, of belonging to the universe as a whole, combined with a strong feeling of awe and wonder and with respect for a humanitarian and ecological ethics, then there cannot be any dichotomy between spirituality and science, nor between science and a religion that has such spiritual experiences at its core. (Capra and Luisi, 2014, p. 282)

We can credit research findings from the hard sciences for many of the foundations of current systems theory. In fact, it was a chemist (James Lovelock) and a biologist (Lynn Margulis) who conceived a controversial hypothesis in the 1970s that the Earth is a self-regulating system unto itself. This means that all living things coevolve with their environments and interact with their surroundings to make the system go. This theory, known as the Gaia hypothesis, influenced the philosophies of deep ecology.

This gets to the very nature of human systems, and that brings us back to the Greeks. The soul was provided a special rank that was unique to human existence. Think of the separation of mind and soul like the difference between memorizing something and actually knowing it, or the difference between knowledge and wisdom. Actually, some philosophers saw the soul as part of a grand force that moved the entire universe. Plato even gave it a name—*anima mundi*. The world soul (Capra and Luisi, 2014).

Within our current corporate and political context, we lack a world soul. Unique to human experience is the ability to discover wisdom, which is much more than simple knowledge. Wisdom is often defined as the right use of knowledge, as the use of knowledge for the good of others. Wisdom as a virtue. If this is our definition, then we have a ways to go in discovering our souls.

EMPOWERMENT MATTERS: THE DEEP ECOLOGY OF PEOPLE

With all due respect to Plato, the world could use some soul right about now. Human beings are so conditioned by the mechanisms of the modern age that we struggle to conceive of a world formed from shared experiences and interconnectedness. These beliefs manifest themselves in our day-to-day actions and structures, both at work and in our personal lives. In fact, we are so inclined to linear thinking that nonlinear solutions give us pause (even heartburn).

This may explain why so many of us are bent on controlling each and every facet of our lives, from our calendars to our careers. Even our characterization of chaos as a bad thing and order as a good thing is an example of a linear construct that is hard to shake. Come to think of it, it is fair to wonder if our control issues are conditioned behaviors and not really natural ones.

In large part, we have a lifetime of strict hierarchies to thank for this. No matter our backgrounds and vocations, we all have experience working within similar bureaucracies that preach authority, order, and efficiency. This kind of rationalism provides for clear definitions of each employee's worth in relation to others and clear distinctions for workers in obeying their managers. This is known as a centralized methodology. Individuals may have good ideas, but the organization knows best. People may be smart, but only the system is wise. The same things are found within our schools.

The path forward for leaders and managers of any organization is the same one available to education. Giving voice to people. Widening the system. Interconnectedness. Common understanding. Cultural relevance. This might be best described as the deep ecology of people. Across the wide landscape of corporations, nonprofits, political action groups, and civic organizations, there is a call to action for new structures that are *people-centered* and *purpose-seeking*.

Let us be clear on this point. Great leaders matter greatly, but no leader can adequately improve a system alone. No one person has the authority to fix things because no one person is a match for the system itself. In their work on developing networked organizations, Allen and Cherrey (2000) make the following claim:

> In the constantly changing networked world, individuals in positions of authority do not have enough power to influence because networks do not have a single lever to pull to start the assembly line of change. Nor do positional leaders have enough information to fully understand the whole system. If

leadership capacities are encouraged and developed, anyone in the network can become an agent of leadership. (p. 108)

This is where soulful leadership comes in. Our systems must be participatory. Our leaders must be servant-minded. Within schools and school districts, this is especially critical. We must build school systems that involve people and serve people, because that is the business we are in. Of course, relationships will be key because relationships *are* learning. Betts argues that this shift will require schools to move from a *one-to-many* perspective to a *many-to-one* orientation. In such a system, the teacher is not the sole provider of information, but only one of many (Betts, 1992, p. 41).

The next generation will demand innovations like these because the current system, as constructed, is not enough to get us there. "The inevitable conclusion from the evidence at hand is that the old system is no longer adequate to the task. If we accept this assertion, we must also conclude that no amount of fine-tuning of the old system will produce significant improvement" (Betts, 1992, p. 41).

In the next generation, new systems will be formed that focus on things like engagement and empowerment, relevancy and connectedness. Teachers and students in these types of schools will form their own niches that are self-organized in support of their personal growth and advancement. "There aren't any designers or reengineers to control the flow of information. Information courses rapidly through the organization in its own natural patterns" (Senge, 1999).

Senge encourages leaders to remain open to creative solutions by listening closely to the system, because the system is speaking to us. "Instead of looking for particular leverage points, a living systems thinker might listen for where the system wants to go. By amplifying or intensifying people's overall awareness of that direction, new behaviors will naturally emerge, and propel the overall pattern of the system across the threshold into a new form" (Senge, 1999, p. 144).

MAKE NO MISTAKE: LEADERSHIP MATTERS

We have learned that true systems are organic, symbiotic, and built from the center out. They may appear to outsiders to be chaotic but only to the untrained eye. There is a vibrant system in place and it is being executed with the finest precision, even with input from so many people, even among all that professional collaboration and intellectual debate.

This is why true systems do not really "run themselves." They just appear that way to the outsider. Somebody is always, always making things go. No matter what organizations and schools look like some day, no matter how they evolve and flourish in the new age, leadership will still matter. This is a universal truth, a historical certainty. Let us return to our spirituality metaphor in making this point.

It is quite difficult, even among the most skeptical of us, to gaze upon the unimaginable beauty of the universe and not believe that everything is connected in some magical, mystical way, and that quite possibly somebody is in charge. It is hard to look around, to take in all that we see, and then make an argument that all of this is simply the result of some happenstance of history, some coincidence of science, or some accident of time.

The same can be said for great schools and school districts. Though there are very few absolutes in the work that we do, let us be clear about this one. In great schools and great school districts, there is somebody making things go. If that is so, this means that *you* matter.

And lest some of us think that the school or school district down the road has just been lucky or fortunate to have the success it is having, we would be wrong. Something special is happening there because of the people in charge. This is why systems appear to run themselves, because they are rooted in core actions that are founded by core beliefs.

This never changes, no matter the new plans or processes being proposed. In fact, great systems are not really plans nor processes. The system itself is making things go. Plans and processes are not the system; they simply flow from it. We have learned from this text that lasting change always begins with a strong core, a headspring, from which all ideas flow.

This is why soulful leadership is needed now more than ever. Authentic leadership. Servant leadership. It is what the world needs badly, and schools do as well. As promised, the world will call on leaders in the new generation who have strong core beliefs and who live out those beliefs through word and deed. Not just sort of, not just kind of, but actually and genuinely.

Maslow describes this as the difference between *being* something and *trying to be* something. "Anybody who puts on behavior like a cloak, as an actor would, finds that this doesn't work very well. People somehow are able to detect at some conscious level or unconscious level that a person is acting and not really feeling deeply the attitude which he is trying to convey through his behavior" (Maslow, Stephens, and Heil, 1998, p. 105).

We can think of this like the difference between knowledge and wisdom, between managing and leading. The future will demand that our leaders, like our systems, remain nimble and forward-thinking. Highly competent and highly connected. Enlightened and empowering. Always prepared to take the system where it has never been before. As Albert Einstein so presciently stated: "We cannot solve our problems with the same thinking we used when we created them."

As leaders with great influence and little time, we alone must decide how bold we will be in daring a new way forward, in determining the casualties of our own making and the triumphs of our own desires. In his classic tome *The*

Art of War, Sun Tzu writes: "When I let go of what I am, I become what I might be."

No matter what becomes of the boy in the back row, his future will not arrive as some accident of time or place. It will happen for him as it has for every other, as a life fashioned from the designs of our own doing. Until then, he will remain there in that place, among so many like him, dreaming the lives of others and staring at a girl whose name he does not know.

Afterword

A Note on Leadership

There is no way that we can be certain of the shape and form that our schools will take someday. The world is moving so fast that even a book on the topic may not get everything right. Still, what will never change in our industry and every other one is the need for inspired leadership. In fact, it is the thing that has always mattered most. If you don't believe me, you can ask Maslow the next time you see him.

This is meant to say that we owe the next generation the best that we have, and that we are never going to make the kind of impact we are capable of without our best leaders in place. I say this because leading in the new age will require something special in our young leaders that is becoming harder to find among the aggressiveness of modern politics and the crudeness of social commentary.

In selecting a descriptor that fits best, we will turn to servant leadership. Ethical. Genuine. Authentic. Positive. Yes, even spiritual. This is not to say that leaders must be religious, per se, but that we not quell our thirst for the spirituality that compels us all. Maslow calls this kind of leadership "enlightened":

> Enlightened management is one way of taking religion seriously, profoundly, deeply, and earnestly. . . . For those who define religion not necessarily in terms of the supernatural, or ceremonies, or rituals, but in terms of deep concern with the problems of human beings, with the problems of ethics, of the future of man, then this kind of philosophy, translated into the work of life, turns out to be very much like the new style of management and of organization. (Maslow, Stephens, and Heil, 1998, p. 82)

Of course, this deep concern for others begins by recognizing the goodness in others, even trusting in good intent when others remain skeptical. If you struggle with such things, I would encourage you to visit a school and take note of the children there. Go ahead. Look deep into the eyes of the children there, deep into the recesses of their souls. If you do, you will see goodness and only that. You will see purity and innocence and hope—the fragrance of spring.

We see this even in the eyes of troubled kids, the ones we may not want as our own. If we look past their behaviors for a moment, we will see goodness in them as well. I know this because I have seen it time and time again—as a parent, teacher, and leader across many, many schools. Like you, I have spent my life encountering young people.

Teachers will tell you the same things if you ask them. For they know best. They encounter children each day the way a poet encounters words, the way a sailor knows the sea. Throughout my life, I have witnessed good prevail over evil countless times. Like you, I have seen the death of winter give way to the fragrance of spring.

These encounters have given me a sense of the inherent goodness of people, no matter how naïve that sounds. I say this because there is a recurring truth and defining quality among great leaders that cannot be understated: they seek to serve not themselves but others. In fact, it was Mahatma Gandhi who said it best: "The best way to find yourself is to lose yourself in the service of others."

I am willing to bet that if we could pinpoint the absolutes that define strong leadership, we would find goodness at the core. We would find honest-to-God goodness among our best leaders. Yes, it is true. Not all leaders have this quality, but the best ones do. Without it, leaders become what we see too often—self-serving, power-hungry, rudderless.

Our postmodern manners have given rise to ethical decision-makers who situationalize, marginalize, and rationalize every move—no matter how unctuous their decisions may be. When this happens, we suffer the consequences of the foolish (that would be us) and turn our moral authority over to the feckless (that would be them).

After many years serving at the command of great leaders, I have come to learn that leadership is the process of making rightful decisions and navigating the fallout from them. Not making decisions is easy, of course. Watching from the sidelines and critiquing the decisions of others is easier still. And so it goes in the life of leaders in organizations both large and small.

As leaders, we cannot pick and choose our decisions like we're squeezing a tomato at the market. Nothing is ever quite that easy. No matter how small, almost all decisions are ethical ones. Once we get beyond the black-and-white decisions around which color of paper to print the brochure on or whether the buses should enter through the north or south gate, we find ourselves mired in ethical messes.

Which child is permitted to turn an assignment in late (or not)? Which child is being suspended (or not)? Which child are we shuffling to the next grade without the proper skills to succeed? Which young person will we allow to walk in the final hours leading to graduation? When do we round up or down? When do we look the other way? When do we make a scene?

Yes, all of the hard questions are ethical ones, made among a milieu of skepticism and in full view of the critics. These decisions are shaped by many forces and become clashes of ethical principles and core values. Among the variables in play are district policies, our allegiance to our bosses and coworkers, and our own professional liability.

Certainly, we are hired to interpret and follow policy and we can't have leaders in place who just make stuff up. Still, we have all seen decisions made that are not in service to children and then watched quietly as leaders blamed some policy for its harsh requirements. Of course, in our line of work, the final outcomes at stake are personal and affective. Our students, their families, their futures. This is where the ethics of fairness and virtue come into play. Once we realize that these situations are not being played out in a textbook, decisions become much more difficult. Lives are impacted.

Most leaders cannot separate their work lives and decisions from their personal ones, and that is a good thing. Like many of you, I believe firmly that we are who we are and those qualities underpin the decisions we make as leaders. Yes, we all mature. We might even soften (or harden) a bit over time, but most of us are who we were raised to be, and that person will come through in the toughest of times.

When I was a child, my father taught me many, many things. He was the kind of person who could fix just about anything. He could even cook and clean, in large part because my mother passed away at a young age. I can still recall Dad's exacting directions when it came to cleaning my room, especially the particulars about how one should crease and tuck the corners of the bed sheets at just the right angles.

In those days, Dad even taught me how to vacuum and dust properly. In fact, I spent every Saturday morning of my life vacuuming and dusting, not that I am bitter about it. The point here is that he taught me early on to work hard at what I do and to do it well. In fact, I can recall with some clarity his insistence that I move the vase when I dusted. It was the only proper way to do it. In this family, we don't dust around the vase. We don't take shortcuts.

So, here's the thing that I mean to say. If we want to make our schools and school districts the best in the world, we can't take shortcuts. At the end of the day, leadership is gaining the trust in those we serve that we are never going to dust around the vase, even when no one is looking. This is something they don't teach you in graduate school.

This is spiritual. This is ethical.

As for the research on ethics, I am not buying it so much. It attempts to outline and quantify ethical decision-making as if it were a five-step plan—like a list of dos and don'ts in a hurricane survival guide. Nearly all of the decisions I have faced are either too complex for that or must be resolved too quickly for that kind of deliberation and study.

We should know that people are watching and listening very closely. That is why I submit that ethical leaders must first be genuine, meaning that leaders should be upfront with their thinking and decisions, even their agendas. In this way, being ethical is akin to being real.

In the postmodern age, we are surrounded by too many self-serving leaders. Worse yet, we find many who seek to "get ahead" without being willing to work very hard or learn very much. These leaders operate in formal and informal ways to undermine the virtues of organizations and individuals. They even teach others that getting ahead at all costs is an accepted practice.

I reject that notion.

As naive as it sounds, I believe that great organizations are built *as* servants and *by* servants. Though we have sometimes strayed from this model, servant leadership is in great demand as we enter a new age. The people I encounter in my life and workplace are eager to be led, to be supported, and to be celebrated. They are fully prepared to be inspired, if only there was something worthy of it. Though our nature causes us to serve ourselves first, our virtue causes us to serve others. We are never fully satisfied unless both callings are clear.

In a speech to students at Tubingen University in Germany many years ago, former British prime minister Tony Blair called on young people to "resolve an apparent conflict between old and new, modernizers and traditionalists." He said: "The resolution of this conflict lies in applying traditional values to the modern world; to leave outdated attitudes behind; but rediscover the essence of traditional values and then let them guide us in managing change. The theologians among you will say it is reuniting faith and reason."

So there it is: faith and reason as antecedents to leadership. It's a good starting point for any young person. We have learned from a long trail of failures that our society doesn't need more blind rule-followers or policy wonks. We have too many of those already.

We need leaders who bring authenticity and positivism to work each day and help others to share in it. In truth, it is tough to remain positive in an age of critics—to suffer what we might describe as the great pangs of positivism. In fact, it is easier to give in to the pressures of unsavory leadership in an unseemly world.

Let this be a challenge to our young leaders to rage against this attitude and stand firm in the face of the ethical pressures they will face. The future will require those who are willing to suffer the pangs of positivism, who trust in the mercy of the many, and who dance in the delight of a new dawn. We need those who have watched the jubilant sun pierce even the darkest clouds. We need those who have seen goodness and hope in the eyes of young children.

So let us suffer the pangs of positivism. Let us be naïve in the face of the critics. Let us be hopeful and ethical and servant-minded.

If we cannot, then let us be imbeciles in a world of madmen.

References

Allen, Kathleen, and Cynthia Cherrey. 2000. *Systemic Leadership: Enriching the Meaning of Our Work*. Lanham, MD: University Press of America.
Banathy, Bela. 1991. *Systems Design of Education: A Journey to Create the Future*. Englewood Cliffs, NJ: Educational Technology Publications.
———. 1992. *A Systems View of Education: Concepts and Principles for Effective Practice*. Englewood Cliffs, NJ: Educational Technology Publications.
Betts, Frank. 1992. "How Systems Thinking Applies to Education." *Educational Leadership* 50, no. 3: 38–41.
Bronson, Po, and Ashley Merryman. 2010. "The Creativity Crisis." *Newsweek*, July 12, 2010.
Capra, Fritjof. 1996. *The Web of Life: A New Scientific Understanding of Living Systems*. New York: Doubleday.
———. 2000 [1975]. *The Tao of Physics: An Exploration of the Parallels between Modern Physics and Eastern Mysticism*. Boston: Shambhala Publications.
Capra, Fritjof, and Pier Luisi. 2014. *The Systems View of Life: A Unifying Vision*. Delhi: Cambridge University Press.
Covey, Stephen. 2004. *The 8th Habit: From Effectiveness to Greatness*. New York: Free Press.
Curtis, Rachel, and Elizabeth City. 2015. *Strategy in Action: How School Systems Can Support Powerful Teaching and Learning*. Cambridge, MA: Harvard Education Press.
De Geus, Arie. 1997. *The Living Company: Habits for Survival in a Turbulent Business Environment*. Boston: Harvard Business School Press.
Despres, Blane. 2004. "Systemic Thinking and Education Leadership: Some Considerations." *International Electronic Journal for Leadership in Learning* 8, no. 7.
Dewey, John. 2004 [1916]. *Democracy and Education*. Mineola, NY: Dover Publications.
Friedman, Thomas. 2006. *The World Is Flat*. New York: Farrar, Straus and Giroux.
Hollister, Rose, and Michael Watkins. 2018. "Too Many Projects." *Harvard Business Review*, September–October.
Kliebard, Herbert. 2004. *The Struggle for the American Curriculum—1893–1958*. New York: RoutledgeFalmer.
Maslow, Abraham. 1959. *New Knowledge in Human Values*. New York: Harper & Row.
Maslow, Abraham, Deborah Stephens, and Gary Heil. 1998. *Maslow on Management*. New York: John Wiley.
Meadows, Donella. 2008. *Thinking in Systems: A Primer*. Edited by Diana Wright. White River Junction, VT: Chelsea Green.
Senge, Peter. 1990. *The Fifth Discipline: The Art and Practice of the Learning Organization*. New York: Doubleday.

———. 1999. *The Dance of Change: The Challenge of Sustaining Momentum in Learning Organizations*. New York: Doubleday.

Sze, David. 2017. "Maslow: The 12 Characteristics of a Self-Actualized Person." Life (blog), *Huffington Post*, December 6, 2017. Accessed March 3, 2019. www.huffpost.com/entry/maslow-the-12-characteris_n_7836836.

Tate, William. 2009. *The Search for Leadership: An Organizational Perspective*. West Dorset, UK: Triarchy Press.

Wenger, Etienne, and Beverly Wenger-Trayner. 2015. "Communities of Practice: A Brief Introduction." April 15, 2015. Accessed March 3, 2019. http://wenger-trayner.com/wp-content/uploads/2015/04/07-Brief-introduction-to-communities-of-practice.pdf.

Wheatley, Margaret, and Myron Kellner-Rogers. 1998. "Bringing Life to Organizational Change." *Journal for Strategic Performance Measurement* (April–May): 1–12.

Wood, Johnny. 2018. "Children in Singapore Will No Longer Be Ranked by Exam Results. Here's Why." October 11, 2018. Accessed March 3, 2019. www.weforum.org/agenda/2018/10/singapore-has-abolished-school-exam-rankings-here-s-why.

About the Author

Daniel J. Evans is an award-winning teacher, school principal, researcher, and writer in one of the nation's largest and most innovative school districts. He is the author and creator of an engaging school leadership blog (www.instructionalsoul.com) that is dedicated to helping educators infuse innovative approaches to teaching and learning. He has a loyal social media following where he dispenses his fresh and inspiring takes on education policy and practices.

Dan currently serves as the executive director for assessment, accountability, and research for his school district on Florida's west coast. He has worked previously as a high school English teacher, school principal, and adjunct professor of education.

He was most recently a high school principal for five years in St. Petersburg, Florida, where he was asked by the superintendent to take over a school that earned a D grade from the state for seven consecutive years and was placed under state watch as a "turnaround" school. During his tenure, the school earned a B grade for the first time in its history and was removed from the state's watch list. As a result of his accomplishments, the school district honored him with the Principal Achievement Award for Outstanding Leadership and nominated him for the state's principal of the year award.

Dan has served as his district's supervisor for secondary reading/literacy and worked for many years as a speaker, trainer, and consultant for other school districts. Dan is a devoted researcher in the areas of systems theory and complexity theory, and he is an ardent educational historian. He has a bachelor's degree in journalism from the University of Florida, a bachelor's degree in English from Florida Atlantic University, and both a master's degree and doctorate in educational leadership from the University of South Florida. He lives with his wife and teenage son in sunny Florida.

www.ingramcontent.com/pod-product-compliance
Lightning Source LLC
Chambersburg PA
CBHW021851300426
44115CB00005B/118